ENTERING
THE WORLD OF
MULTI-DIMENSIONAL
HEALING

Energetic Healing with the Angels, Dragons,
Fairies and Spirit Animals

Lois
Thank you for
Joining me on
this Magical !!
Journey.
♡ Blessings.
K. Buckler

Instructor & Holistic Practitioner
Kimberley Anne Buckler

LOIS DUKE
1716 10 AVENUE NE
CALGARY AB
T2E 0Y1

Tellwell Talent
www.tellwell.ca

ISBN
978-0-2288-2213-4 (Paperback)
978-0-2288-2214-1 (eBook)

TABLE OF CONTENTS

INTRODUCTION

This book was brought forth by the realization that another story needed to be told. In my world, these stories are true. As many of you read this book, you will realize that you, too, have had many experiences that are similar and the events that I get to share will be affirmations for you.

When we are children we get to play in the world of imagination, where things are seen, and words and songs are heard. Stories are told and we sometimes have invisible friends. Our friends may be spirits, fairies, dragons, trolls, elves, pixies or spirits. When we can visit our (imaginary) spirit friends, we are happy and able to access the realms that many have shut out by closing the doors. Maybe we were a bit frightened, or someone kept telling us that these things are not real and only our imagination. It may take an uncluttered mind or a pure heart to be able to access these realms, and when we do, the magic really begins.

Join me on this journey of the heart and soul to see what is here for us to experience and become open to the other dimensions again. As an energy worker, from helping humankind and animals heal within to helping spirits cross over to the other side, the universe opened its doors to me to see and remember who we really are.

My first book is called, *"The Essence of Who We Are" A Guide to Understanding Who We Are: Body, Heart,* Spirit *and Soul.*

My second book is called, *"Essentials for Natural Healing" Healing for the Whole Body: Emotional, Mental, Physical, Spirit* and *Soul.*

I have been involved in holistic work since 2002 as a Reiki Master/Instructor. From 2001 to the present, have been providing energy sessions while accessing the different dimensions and working with my helpers and team, doing intuitive readings, Akashic record healing, house clearings and teaching a few workshops. The students and I get to learn and share together as we all work to provide a healthier world and well-being within.

Dedication

Over the years I have had a lot of support from amazing fellow practitioners in my field. I want to thank everyone who walked this journey with me and brought affirmations to what I have seen, heard and felt. As I journeyed through all of this, I got to share and teach that there are so many possibilities and ways to heal our bodies, homes and land.

Thank you to all the clients and practitioners who trusted me and reached out when they had no answers. I am both blessed and honoured that we could all work together to create a healthier world.

Huge thank you to my soul family for having my back and showing up as we needed each other. This lifetime on Mother Earth has been very magical.

Thank you, Johno, who provided me with a safe place to be along the dragon lei line in Australia where this book got anchored in. Thank you for taking me to the land and cave where we once lived with more of our soul family.

Thank you to Hillory who helped me to get this book started and the affirmation that it was to be written. You are amazing and I am very blessed to be able to work with you.

Thank you, Fabian, for letting me see your dragon in detail, and giving me a safe place to write my book. It has been a huge pleasure to work with you and very grateful for the things we both learnt in this lifetime.

www.spirit-soul-healing.com

CHAPTER 1

Our Soul and Different Dimensions

March 11, 2018
When I was walking down the stairs to the main level at my friends'
house to make a coffee in the morning, I got a strong feeling that I was
to write a third book and knew that it was to be anchored in while in
Australia. As soon as I felt this, I got a huge truth shiver. I was not quite
sure what this book was to be about, but knew my trip here got the book
anchored in for me. At this time, I also realized that Australia was my
place of huge energetic activations. During my first visit in 2010 was
when the animal spirits started to come visit me during dream time. This,
I will share later in the book.

This visit in March of 2018 led me to go through my journal and highlight the experiences that I have had over the years that occurred during healing sessions and in daily life. All of this is known as natural healing while accessing different dimensions of time and space.

What has drawn me to natural healing and sharing my experiences?

I have seen and still see so many people, including myself, who have struggled for survival and wonder if they are really connected to "Source". Over the years, the following questions started to come to my mind:

- What is self-worth?
- Did we have previous lives?
- Why are we not getting it?
- Why do people believe their healing is done when they are just starting?
- Are we holding on to threads of anger?
- Who are we hiding from? Are we hiding from others? Is it our true self we are hiding from?
- Can we be a fairy in one life then a human in the next? Or can we be both and be coexisting in both dimensions simultaneously?
- Are angels, fairies and dragons real?
- Are our setbacks poetic justice from another life? Or do we need to heal from the setbacks that we experience?
- What if we do not take accountability for our actions and we lash out at others?
- Do we have a purpose? What does our heart ache to do? What is stopping us from doing it?

With these questions, we can get the answers by connecting energetically to our bodies and surroundings. Through accessing energy work, psychic readings, and using foods and herbs as medicines, we have all sorts of ways of natural healing.

How our soul can have many stories to tell.

A soul can tell many stories of existence, from the beginning of the time of the soul to present time. This may be ten years to thousands of years. Even a newer soul has stories to tell and experiences to share. Souls can be from different dimensions and have various levels of vibration. These levels of vibration help them to coexist on the planet that they are from or in the dimension that they are existing in. This soul may appear as an angel, animal, dragon, fairy, human or a being from another planet.

Some souls were created by God/Creator to help in other galaxies in the universe and other planets, and to bring knowledge forward to share. Or maybe a soul was created to create beauty where it is living through art or music. Each soul operates on many different vibrational levels, depending on what dimension or planet it originated from.

I have seen souls come from other planets, operating in multiple dimensions, and those that are pure love and light as they have not yet been affected by the existence of humankind. There are souls that are here to learn or to be of service that come to earth pure of heart, then, unfortunately, have their energy affected by the lives of the family they were brought into. Maybe they choose this family for this reason and to learn new lessons that this planet and existence can offer.

Information about our souls can be found in the Akashic records located in the Universal Library. This is in the eighth dimension, and we will explore this later in the book.

This brings forward the need to work on a multidimensional level for healing within.

Our soul and spirit can experience many lives on different planets, including Mother Earth. Some of the things that occur in different lifetimes include:

1. A soul may or may not continue with the same human bloodline.

   - The soul could reincarnate back into the same human family.
   - The soul could choose another family to come back and work with.

2. The soul may choose a different nationality to experience different cultural lessons.

   - The soul may choose to be born into a Scottish family in its first life, then into an Asian family in its next life.

3. Souls start off as amazing love and light; the soul is pure of love, but it can be affected by the following:

   - A soul may not be able to recalibrate its DNA or vibrational level properly before getting here. This state of vibration can leave the body of the human body in a state of discomfort during its lifetime or future lifetimes until a recalibration is done energetically.
   - DNA may be recalibrated or damaged by using chemicals, causing harm to the human body and leaving imprints on the soul line.
   - A soul may be told to forget who it was so that it can function on earth, as it is subject to the standards or beliefs of those around it during each lifetime. (I remember being told this same thing, though I could not remember what lifetime I heard it. Was told to forget who I was, so that I would be safe.)
   - A soul can be traumatized by harsh events that occurred during a lifetime. The soul can be fragmented until healed again.

- The spirit of the soul can be stuck on the earth plane due to extreme physical and/or mental damage during its life as a human or animal.
- The spirit of the soul can get lost or become quite dark due to unhealthy practices or beliefs.

There are many souls that originated from another planet or from the beginning of time that come to earth to help with the ascension, bringing humankind back to the state of oneness, to live in bliss. These souls are helping to share and teach the origins of our being. We are now able to reteach humankind that we are God's/Creator's energy and pure love and light within. We have love within us that is so strong it can transmute diseases and discomforts that the human body holds on to.

Learning to work with multiple dimensions.

The first time I stepped in my healing room that was set up for clients, I prepared myself and asked for protection, not fully understanding what I was setting into place. I would say, "Please provide me with guidance and protection during this healing. Only those of the love and light are welcome in this room." As I become aware that we can heal human and animal bodies along with the spirit and the soul on a vibrational level, I started to understand that the healing can be found within different dimensions. The energy/vibration of each dimension varies in density, temperature, energy and knowledge. It was many years later that I fully understood what I was doing during the treatments and how my helpers were from the different dimensions. I knew that I was working with angels, the animal kingdom, the Fairy Realm, the light beings and my teachers from my home planet.

When I was first exposed to the Fairy Realm, the bottom of my legs got cold. A few years later, when I felt the energy of an elf, who was quite tall, the whole right side of my body got freezing cold. If there was something for a person to learn at the time, messages would come from the animal kingdom or from the angels. When I felt the energy of the Akashic records, my body heated up. Temperatures and vibrations seemed to vary with each dimension, and I believe that this was in order to get my attention and help me understand the difference in the energies and who was with me.

The purpose of this book is to share who we are working with, even though we are on the earth plane. No, I am not crazy, as the information that I am sharing has been acknowledged by many other practitioners around the world and even in some churches. Shamans, healers, Christians and many others who have seen and shared stories like these ones for thousands of years. Those who are afraid create stories that have harmed many practitioners by trying to stop us from doing the work that we were born to do. Some of the harm directed at natural healers is caused by fear that is instilled by churches, which say that healers are witches and are working with the devil. Yet the fearmongering groups cause more heavy energy and diseases that are necessary to feed the egos of those who want power. Now is the time to share what is really going on around us and how we can bring positive change and healing to Mother Earth and her inhabitants.

The different dimensions as I am starting to understand them.

When first starting this book, the goal was to be able to distinguish between the different dimensions and understand what each dimension contained. As I began my research, there were so many conflicting stories, and the information I gathered got jumbled and I got confused. I had to walk away from the book for a bit and re-evaluate how to approach it, as this information is still being gathered and humans are once again getting a grasp on what has been here with us for thousands of years. Much of this information was lost during the transition of religious movements and wars that damaged written knowledge and research.

The **first step** is to share some of the different energies and groups that I have worked with, both knowingly and unknowingly. As the book progresses, I will explain how we can access these energies and helpers that are here with us each day.

Some of the groups that I work with include:
Angels
The Animal Kingdom: spirit animals, totem animals and animals with physical bodies
Alien Energies: energy that comes from other planets and solar systems
Crystal Energies
Dragons and Dragonfae
Elements: Air, Earth, Fire and Wind
Fairies: brownies, elves, fairies, gnomes, goblins, leprechauns, mermaids, nymphs, pixies, sprites and unicorns are all part of the Fairy Realm
Light Beings
Plant Medicine

The **second step** is to learn about some of the ways that I get to see and experience the above.

There are 12 known different dimensions, and I have a feeling there are many more that we are unaware of. During my research, I found that some of these energies/groups exist in different dimensions while some are found in the same one. My goal is to share stories about the experiences that I have had during my sessions with clients, while travelling and while doing house and land clearings.

CHAPTER 2

The 12 Dimensions, Chakras and What We Can Access for Healing

A few years ago, a dear friend shared with me that we have 12 chakras. Even though some say that the chakra system has changed, I am staying with what was shared with me. As I gathered information on the dimensions, I realized that they are in sync with our 12 chakras.

We are also taught that we have seven basic chakras: root, sacral, solar plexus, heart, throat, third eye and crown. The root chakra is connected to the earth plane. The vibration of the root chakra is different than that of the crown charka, the crown being connected to our Source /God/Creator.

1st Dimension

Chakra: Root
Main state of well-being: survival - home, food, clothing
Location: pelvic area

- This 1st dimension is known as awareness.
- This is where we find the energies of the mineral kingdom and water.
- The human body survives in this dimension as its DNA is calibrated to survive here on planet Earth.
- Its elements are: Air, Earth, Fire and Wind
- Associate with this dimension are: Blue Rays

2nd Dimension

Chakra: Sacral
Main state of well-being: emotional, sexuality
Location: by our belly button

- The 2nd dimension is the energies of the plants of Mother Earth and, from what I've read, is known as the lower animal kingdom.
- This is the space where there is the need to create and procreate, eat, and where one must fight to survive.
- This dimension is about feeling the awareness of the moment. To be able to feel the emotions that are associated with life circumstances.
- For the human, this dimension affects the lower brain that works with the autonomic nervous system, helping to maintain and regulate the functions of the body.

- Associated with this dimension: Aquarians, plant and animal lovers.

3rd Dimension

Chakra: Solar Plexus
Main state of well-being: mind, intuition, humans and higher animals
Location: by the junction at the bottom of our ribcage

- The 3rd dimension consists of time and space: point, line, breadth and width, height and volume.
- This is where humans and the higher animal kingdom reside.
- This dimension has to do with the awareness of oneself, but it also comes with the ability to be aware, of the connection with others around us.
- This is where a person is focused on oneself and hard work.
- When a person is stuck in this state of well-being, they are not able to remember their past or past lives.
- This dimension is where the human soul can be stuck due to cause and effect and/or time and space. This can be carried forward into future lives and timelines.

4th Dimension

Chakra: Heart
Main state of well-being: to love oneself
Location: heart area

- The 4th dimension is known as the astral plane and astral body/etheric. This is the space of Universal Law.
- This involves a higher state of being; to become aware of our unconscious mind.

- The astral body carries a higher vibration than that of the physical body.
- The state of the unconscious mind includes advanced dreaming, dreaming, imagination, intuition, magic and psychic ability.
- This dimension is about understanding that we all are connected and that our actions have a ripple effect.
- The Indigos hold this awareness, which helps them to access multiple dimensions and practise healing of the earth and humankind. This group is helping humankind and Mother Earth to heal.
- This is the state where ego does not resonate and where we know that we are one and no one person is better than the other.
- Related to this realm: Buddha, astral planes and astral projection, Atlanteans, humanity, Universal Law and One-Consciousness.

5th Dimension

Chakra: throat
Main state of well-being: the ability to communicate with ease
Location: throat area

- The 5th dimension is known as the possible worlds where the spirit exists, and where time and space do not bind consciousness.
- There is no sense or any illusion of being separated or limitations. A sense of oneness reigns. I AM.
- This realm is known as heaven: the Realm of Goodness. These are the people/spirits that have the essence of kindness and gentle ways. They are filled with compassion and are humble, pure of heart and very loving. They are the ones that will send blessings of joy, peace and well-being.

- This realm is about unconditional forgiveness and unconditional love; this is a state of acceptance.
- This realm does not hold any anger, judgment, guilt or negativity. This feels like being in the Akashic records.
- Here, we are can create freely and the creating will be coming from the oneness, unity consciousness.
- Related to this realm: the Etheric Template, Lemurians, planets, the ability to transcend time and space.

6th Dimension

Chakra: third eye

Main state of well-being: To be able to see into the other dimensions, to use our psychic abilities, to know that our imagination can be real and that the things we see are possible

Location: forehead

- The 6th dimension is the Realm of Light, the plane of all possible worlds. The Crystal Children or Magical Children are from this realm. They know how they can automatically use magic or access the other realms. They are very playful and know how to enjoy life. They can create with ease.
- These are lovingly empowering and compassionate leaders; they teach the love and kindness that are part of this realm.
- This dimension is about being able to see the blessings in life and to acknowledge them so that others see them, too.
- Those that excel in this realm rise to a higher level, which is the state of Arhat: the start of being one. They are training as angels or Bodhisattvas and are furthering their spiritual training.
- Associated with this dimension: angels and those with divine missions.

7th Dimension

<u>Chakra:</u> Crown
<u>Main state of well-being:</u> knowledge, understanding, spiritual connection, wisdom, a higher etheric and physical state
<u>Location:</u> above the head

- The 7th dimension is the Angelic Realm or Bosatsu Realm. This is where we reside in true love for all those around us to serve God/Creator and help others heal their spirit and soul. To live the life of love and peace and to bring it forth for others to evolve.
- This is the plane of all possible worlds, each with different start conditions.
- Crystal Adults or Christ-Conscious Adults are those who can bring in and live in the higher-dimension consciousness and initiate healing for others. They have learned to carry this energy in their aura.

8th Dimension

<u>Main state of well-being:</u> transcendence and connection to spirit and earth; accessing higher consciousness
<u>Location:</u> Soul Star Chakra.

- The 8th dimension is known as the Tathagata Realm. The archangels and Bodhisattvas live in this realm. Religious sects and spiritual practices come into being.
- This is the plane of all possible worlds and different start conditions, each branching out infinitely.
- Those from this dimension have expansive knowledge and are free spirits; they can access many levels of the realms.
- When in this dimension, a person can have more control over their life on earth, as they have learned to live with ease and no ego.
- This is also known as the realm of time and space.

- This dimension is connected to parallel universes and lives, Akashic records, and accessing the essence of one's soul. Being able to heal the soul in other timelines/past lives.
- In this dimension, one works with spirit guides.
- This dimension is about bringing in and living within the divine light of "God/Creator" and to live in this energy each day.

9th Dimension

Main state of well-being: spiritual evolution
Location: Seat of the Soul

- The 9th dimension is the Cosmic Realm.
- This dimension is the inclusion of all possible worlds, starting with all possible conditions and laws of physics.
- This dimension incorporates the 8th dimension.
- This is also known as the Realm of Saviours: the ten great spirits that have looked after Mother Earth since it was created. Each of them is a source of the seven-coloured light, which is the essence of the terrestrial spirit group.
- These dimensional beings have silver or white energies
- To be able to reach this dimension is the soul's purpose, the destiny of our life/lives. This is when we have evolved from the chaos that human life can created, and to have learnt all the lessons that we may have come here to learn.
- This dimension is concerned with soul family DNA and coding on a soul level.
- The archetypal energies associated with this dimension: spirit guides, light beings and star beings.

10th Dimension

Main state of well-being: all that is
Location: below the earth's surface

- The 10th dimension is where one has responsibilities of the universe on a solar level. This is the work of angels, dragons and light beings.
- The dimension has infinite possibilities.
- Those dwelling here have gold energies
- In this dimension, one can connect with the divine light beings.
- This dimension allows for light-body integrations, using the Divine Merkabah.
- This dimension is said to be below the earth's surface.
- This dimension is concerned with DNA coding of the human body, and healing of bones, marrow and skeletal construction.
- This dimension is also concerned with the environment.

11th Dimension

<u>Main state of well-being</u>: mind over matter
<u>Location:</u> hand and feet chakras

- The 11th dimension is the Galactic level of consciousness.
- Those residing here have gold, silver, and violet healing energies.
- This dimension encompasses prophecy and accessing the Akashic records, the universe's "Book of Life"
- This dimension allows for the use of advanced spiritual skills, travelling through time and space, and going into the Records to provide healing; healing from all the beings of the light.
- In this dimension one can teleport and communicate with the ascended masters, the great brotherhood of all; the highest vibrational light beings.
- Instant manifestation is possible.
- Those residing here use energy to heal the body emotionally, mentally, physically and spiritually.

- This dimension is about creating magic and shaping matter, as well as bringing balance to humanity, earth and higher realms of spirit.

12th Dimension

Main state of well-being: connected with the universe and Source
Location: heart and soul

- This dimension is also known as the Gold Ray of Universal Consciousness, Unity, and the Divine Gateway.
- This dimension is about becoming a full universal being. Having returned to Source with unity consciousness, with a physical form of our local universe.
- Energies in this dimension are multicoloured orbs of light.
- This is our divine light portal.
- This dimension encompasses unconditional love and compassion; enlightenment.
- This is the doorway to other realms and worlds.
- This dimension represents full ascension; spiritual gifts.
- This dimension is about entering the Super Galactic realms and accessing the Divine Mother and the womb of the universe; becoming one with the Mother.
- Associated with this realm: Goddess of Light, Stargates, and bringing peace, balance and ascension to humanity.

Now that you have a bit of an understanding of how our chakras and the different dimensions are connected, we can take it a step forward.

When we are healing our body, mind and soul, we can go through many shifts, and the changes can come by using a lot of different techniques, along with accessing the ancient knowledge and medicines that we have used in this lifetime or previous lifetimes.

What I get to do with this book is share the many stories of house clearings and the healing work with clients, as well as my experiences working with other realms during these sessions. Other experiences occurred while travelling for work or pleasure. I hope these stories will help you to understand that you are not alone and there is someone here that supports you. When we are learning, it is nice to have a navigation tool that is not a restricted one, but one that gets you to use your intuition and to know that there are many possibilities and outcomes of healing within the different dimensions.

CHAPTER 3

Energy and Spirit Clearings for the Home, Humans and Land

I am going to share some stories about events that I have personally witnessed that bring clarity to humankind and have helped me realize what has happened to humans over thousands of years. These stories include what happens when energy becomes heavy. There are many ways that the energy around us and within us can be changed, going from peaceful to sad and sick.

Humans have been taught to hate and fear others around them and even themselves. This comes from those in high positions who teach others to judge, as well as greed for money and power and the attempt to control others through telling stories and manipulation of lies. Historically, the hate and fear they instilled brought a sense of power to those of high rank, so that they could maintain control of their servants and fellow humankind in their communities and across the land. These power-hungry people did not want humans to have access to the higher realms and God/Creator energies.

For example, in the past, churches taught that only the priest or minister could heal the population. In the present day, doctors are controlled by the churches and/or pharmaceutical companies. Doctors do play an amazing role and can do a lot of amazing things to help the human body, I feel that the doctors and energy healers should be working together.

In truth, we all can heal our bodies to release the energetic imprints that we hold on to, along with using the medicines that Mother Earth offers. Now it is time to face our fears and know that the love and light within us is stronger than ever and that we can heal ourselves, our homes, businesses and land. We can heal the fear that we have been holding on to and release the anger and no longer judge. These energies have become like imprints on our homes, our bodies and on the land.

Spirit clearings for the home, humans and land.

Spirits that are stuck here on the earth can cause a lot of trouble for animals, humans and the land.

From the time that I was a child to about 40 years of age, I would have dreams of old houses filled with antique furniture, and the spirits that roamed their hallways and rooms. It felt like I knew the houses, even though I don't remember entering them in this lifetime. In the dreams, the antique furniture belonged to family members and friends. I had the sense that some of the furniture was gifted to me and not to other family members. It was always a strange feeling being there with the furniture and to see family members who had passed.

In other dreams and in the awake state at night, I would see faces and bodies of spirits of all sizes around my bed. Then I would feel things come up the side of my bed, and whatever it was would try to hurt me. One of the spots they would hurt me was by the funny bone at the right side of my stomach. Something would poke at me, the discomfort was painful, and this energy was not something that was of the light. I would be poked and pushed. I would wake up screaming for my dad. At that time, I did not realize what was going on. These nasty energies that hurt me are known as entities or parasites. I realized that this kind of energy could not go to the other side and my presence stopped them from doing so. I stopped seeing the spirits at nighttime by the time I was 11 or 12. Yet, I could still feel them around me even in the daytime.

Later, I learned from a shaman that as a soul here on Mother Earth, one of my jobs is to help spirits cross over and to help heal their soul as they are leaving the earth plane. Then, a few years after that, I realized that the things that hurt me were what I call parasites and heavy energy entities. These parasites could have been attached to the spirits, and as my energy field cleared the spirits for transitioning, the parasites got left behind. So, as a child and adult I was seeing and feeling two different things.

Lost spirits: they eventually seek help.

When a person leaves this lifetime, the spirit has a choice to stay here, which is not a healthy choice, or to go over to the other side, to heaven. Fear of judgment and anger has caused a lot of spirits to stay earthbound, as they are scared to be judged, or they believe that they are going to go to hell. In my mind, there is no such thing as hell. We can help to heal and shift the spirits that have been stuck on the earth plane for thousands of years.

Spirits can also get stuck here because of denial, not believing that they have died. Or because of someone—another human—holding the spirit back from crossing. Some spirits are held captive by what one would call a soul collector, and this is truly a mean and nasty thing to do. Spirits are sometimes stuck between dimensions due to contracts that were created, or stuck in timelines, and not able to move on. These beings that part of creating the contracts are seeking power and control, which is never of the light and love. We so truly deserve to be able go freely on to our next life without restrictions. As the spirits stay here and linger, over the years, their vibration becomes heavier and meaner. For the practitioner or priest who is helping them to cross, it can make them feel ill or they may smell a rotting smell from the energy.

The shaman shared with me that some souls/humans are like beacons of light that shine a wee bit brighter, and this light helps to assist spirits and those around us make shifts and changes. As one of those holding this volunteer position here on Earth, we need to recognize who we are and also be able to set boundaries. When one is not aware of this ability, one can get tired, drained and become disconnected. One can become depressed, feel anxious and get physically sick. The anxiety, depression and sick feeling come from the distraught spirits; it is hard on us when we do not recognize that these ill feelings are not ours.

Following are some recaps from my first book, *The Essence of Who We Are.*

I will only share a wee bit of the stories from the first book, just as a reminder for us of what is really going on energetically in our space, and how we can shift these heavy energies. Then I will get into some wild house and land clearings that I have done since the first book.

1. My first client with a lost spirit had just come over for a visit. She had been feeling out of sorts for about two weeks, and she was feeling angry. We went to the healing room and I had her lie on the table. Starting with bringing in Reiki energy, I began by asking her questions when I got to her heart area. After a bit, I found out where she picked up the spirit and, in my mind's eye, I saw the place where she was. This spirit made me feel like I was going to throw up, but by bringing in the light energy we were able to help the spirit (healing its energy field and soul) to cross over.

2. I truly believe that demon energies are also lost souls. Demon energies are spirits that made bad choices in their lifetime or over several lifetimes and did not know how to return to the light. They were exposed to greed, excessive drug or alcohol use, or used bad medicine to control others.

A tenant had brought a demon dog into my home. As first when I saw him I was shocked, but I went to the heart centre and started to bring in the love and light. The dog had been exposed to people who were involved with heavy drugs and alcohol. I also believe that the dog had been abused. This can emotionally harm animals in the same way it harms humans.

3. The third example from my first book is that of a client who had picked up a spirit when she was a teenager. She was lonely and the spirit that came to her offered her a sense of companionship. By the time she came to me, the spirit had become heavy and demanding. She was feeling depressed and lethargic. When I did my energy work on her, I did not sense the spirit as it had stayed in her vehicle. It did not want to come into my home. After she got back into her vehicle, the spirit overtook her and her vehicle crashed into the one in front of her. A few days later, we figured out what happened

and escorted the naughty spirit out with Archangel Michael. Archangel Michael is a protector, he works with a team, that helps to escort spirits over to the other side. You could even see him as being a sheriff or knight of the Angels.

The following stories are true. They are real events: spirits are real and when seen by others, it is a huge affirmation.

Fall 2005: Imprint Clearing

During the summer of 2005, I tried to move back to the city, as I had gotten a job there. I had rented a unit in a four-plex for about three months. After living in Cochrane, AB, for over ten years, I did not like the big-city attitude and the neighbours seemed cold and didn't seem to care who lived next to them. When I left the unit to go back to Cochrane, I left some sage and sweetgrass as a blessing for the new renters. This was something I saw someone else do and thought it a wonderful gesture.

In the fall I got a call from the landlord of the unit that I had rented, as he knew that I did house clearings. He had been doing some renovations on a duplex that he had bought and was hoping to move in shortly. Setback after setback made him realize that maybe if he got a clearing done, he would be able to finish the renos. I had not been told anything when I got there and started with the clearing. When I was in the basement, there was one room that made me feel petrified. Scared to be there. This first room took a while to clear and I kept going around it with the sage until the energy shifted. When I came to the last room in the basement, it felt like a safe place. Where a person could safely hide and know that everything would be okay.

Upstairs in the master bedroom, I got goosebumps on my arms. I felt like I needed to watch my back and I was scared. As I smudged and did energy work, the feelings slowly drifted away, and I felt a lot more comfortable. After I got the duplex all cleared, I shared everything I felt in there and knew why the renos were not going well.

The owner told me that when he bought the duplex there was a huge bloodstain on the carpet in the bedroom. Someone tried to get it out, but you could still see where it was. The woman who lived there was in an abusive relationship and had either been killed or badly hurt. This also explained the basement. This is where the woman would hide when the abuser came to the door. She would hide and felt like the second room, where I felt safe, was the place where she could not be seen through the windows.

Later, I heard back from the owner that the rest of the renos went well. He even had me do a clearing for a good friend of his, as he knew that what I was able to do worked well.

October 2016: Spirit Tag-Along While Travelling

When I remembered this event, the irony behind it all gave me quit the chuckle.

In the late summer and early fall of 2016, I got to travel in Australia for three months. I had planned on being there longer, until about March of 2017. Around the end of the month of October, I started to have some weird things happen to me. As I am typing this, I really wonder if it had to do with the spirit that was attached to me.

In Byron Bay, my credit card started to act funny. I had let Visa know that I was travelling, then suddenly it was doing some weird stuff. I went to Nimbin, NSW, a little hippie town north-west of Byron Bay. I had heard of this town and wanted to check it out. Before I went up there, the credit card acted funny at the gas station in Byron Bay. In Nimbin, I found the sweetest coat that I could wear with a dress. The price was awesome! I went to use the card, and it did not work. I called Visa in tears and got it sorted out.

The next day, I headed back toward Brisbane to stay at a friend's place. Since they were going to be gone for the whole weekend, I started back up the coast. I tried to avoid the toll bridges there, and I got lost on the back roads going through the countryside on the east side of Brisbane. Again, I felt hopeless, sad, lost and didn't know where to stop. I could not find a hotel or restaurant that was open. I stopped at the side of the road and started to cry. Why was I on my own? Why was I feeling so lonely? Why was I feeling so disoriented? Where was I?

I turned my car around and headed back to the beach area that I had just seen. The name of the beach was Deception Bay. I got out of the car and checked my space to see who was there. There was a male spirit and I helped him to cross over. I can't remember much more about him, but I instantly knew why I had been having a hard time. I did a clearing and brought my vibration back up again. I felt a hundred times better. The sadness went away and I knew it was time to get back on the road. Right away, I found the road that I needed to get to Noosa Bay.

After about another half hour of driving, knowing that it was getting late, I found a hotel room in Cabooltour, Queensland. I put my suitcase in the room then went for a good walk. I messaged my stepmom to let her know where I had landed. She told me that this was the town that my dad had passed away in. I truly believe that the universe brought me there for final closure, and this was ten years since Dad had left to join the angels. I had a huge talk with Dad in spirit and thanked him for all the blessings that he brought in my life. A lost spirit that I picked up got me lost and depressed, and releasing the spirit brought me to the town that Dad passed away in. A full circle of healing.

2017: Lost Spirits and One Nasty Spirit.

I'm trying to remember when this clearing happened, and I believed it was after I got back from a trip to Australia.

A good friend recommended me to her dad and stepmom. The first time I went out there, an acreage north-east of Calgary, we cleared out a lot of lingering spirits that were looking for help. My friend's stepmom is an amazing gal who spirits go to for help. She is slowly learning how to work with them now. At that time, when I first went there, I picked up on a hunting knife that I saw in a cabinet and knew that a spirit had come with it. When I shared what I saw, the client told me how they had gone on a trip and her husband had bought the knife from an antique store or a fellow who sold knives and guns. The knife had belonged to either a soldier or a native. The knife had seen some action, and not good events either. I believe that the spirit of the owner was attached to the knife. Now, the spirit is in heaven. Just before I left, I got a raunchy, nasty feeling in my stomach. A toxic feeling that made my stomach churn. I suggested that they get their water tested.

The second time I was called out there was to do a clearing for the neighbour's house. My friend was willing to pay to have her neighbour's house cleared as she was scared to go in there to water the plants and feed the cats. She felt like something did not want her there, so she would ask her husband to go over.

When I got there in the morning, I was told that the door blew right off the hinges the night before and flew across the yard. That was a bit unnerving to hear. It took a bit to go down the stairs. In the far corner of the basement was a nasty, mean, heavy energy spirit. The spirit was holding a female spirit and her child spirit captive in the basement with him. I did not see what had happened to the female and child, as I concentrated on bringing up the vibration of all of them. I wondered if the female and child were connected to the male and had been the victims of abuse. The male was not wanting to let go of what he believed was his. Not a healthy way to live. My heart went out to the female and child. The male spirit was bagged with white netting and taken out by Archangel Michael for further processing. The other two spirits were very happy to be free to cross over.

Before I go on, I'm going to share something that I have seen several times. In houses where spirits are drawn to seek shelter, they often seem to gather in the basement. Is this because the basements are closer to the earth energy? These are spirits that don't know where to go and feel unworthy of God/Creator's love and compassion.

When I went upstairs in this house, I could sense a lot of spirits, mostly in the living room. I had a strong feeling that these spirits had been scared of the nasty spirit in the basement and felt safer upstairs. We helped them to cross over and the only other room that felt off was the office. After this clearing, my friend was able to go over, water the plants and feed the cats.

April 2005 – 2018

Sometimes things that we don't expect to happen occur, and we wonder if we are crazy. As time went on, I was able to put the pieces of this puzzle together. Each clearing of this property cleared energies from so many different areas in the homeowners' present and previous lives. I will ascribe names to the clients: Sarah for the mom, Don for the dad, and Mathew for the baby boy.

2017 the first clearing

The first time I went to clear the home for Sarah, she was expecting a baby within three months or less. She looked so healthy and radiant. With the first clearing, what got my attention was an auntie energy close to the living room. I did not like the energy as it felt invasive and not very loving. We cut a cord from the family to the auntie, hoping that she would stay detached from the home. By the dining room table, I could feel the spirits of family members still lingering and I asked them all to give the living family room to breathe. They did not need to be watched over.

2018 the second clearing

The second time I was called to do a clearing at this house, I was in Australia and shared that I would be back to Canada shortly. The client sounded frantic. I forgot to ask Archangel Michael to protect me and the family until I got there. This is something I do as soon as I get a call for a house clearing, just in case. This was one time the just-in-case got out of hand and scared the crap out of me. Right after I got back home, I got a call from my stepmom to tell me that her mom passed away and she was heading to Canada for the funeral service.

Mom stayed at my place for the night, and the next day I drove her into the city to her sister's. On the way into the city, I had a really hard time driving my car and was getting sleepy. I kept asking Archangel Michael to help us be safe and to escort out any spirits if they were around. I successfully dropped off Mom, then headed back to Cochrane. I was on a major road and had stopped for a red light and there was one car in front of me. Was waiting for the light to change when, suddenly, my car gently hit the one in front. I had blacked out behind the wheel. It was spirit energy that put me to sleep. Thank God the car was in front of me, and that there was no damage to either car, I did not cause a serious accident with the traffic who had the green light. I said thank you to God and my guides for saving my butt and everyone else's.

The next day when I went to do the house clearing, I found out why I got attacked. Let me warn you, we are going to go to another level of spirit energy, in another dimension that I still don't quite understand but know to be true. Later, when I shared this story with a fellow practitioner, I got affirmations of this kind of activity, and, fortunately, we can now make changes as humans evolve to a higher state of vibrational energy.

Sarah let me know why she had called. Her little boy, Mathew, now close to eight months old, was not sleeping or eating well. The little guy was in his bedroom when I showed up, having a nap. As soon as I heard this, I got a weird and unsettling feeling, which I will share in a bit.

I always start in the basement, and as with many basements, this is where a lot of lost spirits linger. Archangel Michael, Two Feathers (my spirit guide) and I helped to clear them so they could all go to heaven. When I got to the main floor, there was a vision in the kitchen that surprised me. In the vision, the house owner, Sarah, was dressed in white and stirring something in a big white cauldron. She was a good witch. One that worked for the highest good of all, good medicine. When I came to the living room, I saw in my mind's eye a dark witch, all in black. Not good medicine. The image came and went quickly. I was startled but forgot about it right away. About 20 minutes later, I was upstairs, going toward the master bedroom. This is where I saw a group of witches.

A story unfolded in front of my eyes (or within my mind). I was told by a spirit what had happened in another time or dimension. The youngest witch, overzealous in her effort to get brownie points, did a deed, at the cost of a human. Either it was for brownie points or in exchange for a favour. Somehow, the young witch had gotten a contract made for the soul of a human boy when he reached the age of eight months. This was a powerful human child. One who was capable of providing a lot of good for the planet. The idea was to misuse this child's energy or skills. This was the feeling that I got as I started the house clearing.

Writing this, I got a chill, but I got affirmation from the angels that I am okay and well protected. This energy/spirit has been divinely looked after.

In my mind's eye, I looked at the young witch in my vision and tried to get across that her actions were not acceptable anymore and that she could not claim the soul of an innocent child. Let her know that her contract was being voided. She could not take what was not hers for selfish reasons and without permission. Contracts that she made this way were no longer allowed on this earth plane and those times of power and control were now over. I went to the little boy's room and did a clearing to dissolve any lingering energy so that he was again safe.

Later, when I finished the house clearing using both sage and then sweetgrass for blessings, I went to the kitchen area. The little guy was happily eating his lunch for the first time in a few days. I found out the next day that he slept very well that night and everything was back to normal.

I asked Sarah about witches and shared that she was dressed all in white in my vision. She is a beautiful soul and holds such a loving energy. I felt that I needed to be careful how I shared this information as I did not want her to be in any way insulted. She shared that she had bought some candles from a store in the US. The store sold a lot of articles that could be used for incantations or spells. She wondered if the candles held a bad energy and was wary about using them. I left that decision up to her. Within her soul memories she knew how to clear black magic from objects.

2018 the third clearing

A few months later, I got asked to do a clearing for the house again and to do a mini card reading for Sarah's husband, Don. This time I got another surprise. In the garage, I got to meet Don's gargoyle and Mathew's blue dragon. They were both looking after the house for their human friends. I saw this in a vision as I smudged with the sage. It was a fun story to share with Sarah and Don. Sarah said something that served as an affirmation. I wish I could remember what it was. When I did this clearing, they were thinking of moving to the US for work—there was a position that the hubby was working hard toward.

2018 the fourth and last clearing

In the fall, Sarah sent me an email asking if I could do a house clearing again for her, as they were now in the US and trying to sell the house. Most of the house felt pretty good, until I got to the spare bedroom upstairs. There was one of the witches from before. She wanted to maintain a hold on the house and the family. I could feel her presence and got a sense of the clothing she wore. I explained to her that holding on to a family and a home was wrong. That things needed to be obtained with dignity and respect. Archangel Michael whisked her off right away and was surprised at the intensity of his presence and what he was about to do. He explained to me that this spirit had already had a warning; this was the last straw for her. Now, the universe will help her out in a divine way so that she will learn not to mess with others' lives and well-being. I believe the house sold after this.

November 2016

The family, house and land in this next story will always have my heart and support. The clearing I did here will never be forgotten, and what was magical were all the affirmations I got while doing the clearing.

I got a call from a gal who had taken a workshop from me. We were to go to her friend's land and do a clearing. Sherry picked me up and drove us north of Cochrane and then west. I had never travelled along this country road that we turned on, and we were heading farther into the hills and a lot more trees and bush. It was lush green everywhere and we saw quite a few small farms along the way. We came to the driveway and turned in.

Suddenly, I blurted out that the cows sure did not look happy. Sherry looked at me funny, and I wondered if I was nuts. Oh, well. Our first stop was a house trailer that needed clearing. The energy was not nice in there and I hoped I had done a good job. There was something about the trailer that did not feel right. I think it needed to be retired and was not healthy to be living in anymore. I talked to the homeowner as I was smudging the trailer, and she shared that they were building a bigger house and she kept on coming into problems with the construction. Each time that contractors were supposed to be there to get some work done, the work would get rescheduled. Nothing with the construction seemed to be going right. After finishing the clearing of the trailer, we headed to the house under construction.

We started in the basement. The owner shared how she did the surface of the basement floor on her own. It was a big basement and the floor looked amazing, but the energy felt off. I asked who was living south-east of the property. She said it was the previous owner. What I felt and said was that it seemed someone was still holding on to the property that we were on and did not want it to sell. The previous owner's daughter and husband had been living on the property, but he did not want to sell to them. There was another piece of property that he wanted his family on. What was needed was to do a cord-cutting from the daughter to the land. Once that was done, something really shifted.

The rest of the clearing went well. When I came to the room that was to be for the youngest daughter, I asked if there was a creek on the south part of the property. I shared that I could feel the fairy energy there. Yes, there was a creek, and this was where the daughter spent most of her time playing with the fairies. She would be out there for hours having fun with her spirit friends.

At the end, I shared everything that I saw and felt. Loaded with affirmations, my heart was singing with joy and very excited that we picked up on everything. The owner said she hoped they had the house done by Christmas. I shared that it would be done by March. All the finishing touches were done by March! The home is a magical house now and I love to go visit.

On the way out to the road, my friend Sherry excitedly told me that the cows looked a lot happier! I guess I was not going nutty. Thank goodness for that affirmation!

August 2017: Entity Clearing

I was at work in town, and the store had been quiet that day. In the middle of the afternoon, a woman came in and asked if I knew of anyone who did house clearings. I asked her what was going on and what I heard shocked me and this had me call in Archangel Michael right away. The woman's daughter was being bothered at night and she showed me a picture of her bed sheet. The daughter's bed sheet had been ripped by what appeared to be claws.

The next day I went out to do the clearing, and in the meantime, I'd asked Archangel Michael to contain whatever was in the home and protect the family. I knew that this was not a hoax and the fear was real. When I got to the girl's room with the sage, in my mind's eye, I saw the creature in the bag of white netting. I started to ask the girl when this animal showed up and what she did when it made itself present to her. She said she kept shooing the animal away and telling it to leave her alone. This young woman obviously has the gift to help spirits out, as I do.

I explained to her how when we just shoe spirits away, their energy gets meaner as time goes on and their actions toward us can get a lot more aggressive. She was very lucky that the spirit just ripped her sheets. I don't believe that it would have hurt her; it just was tired of trying to get her attention. As I did the clearing of her room, I shared with her how to help the spirits out so that this did not happen again. I let her know that she was a beautiful beacon of light and that it was a blessing to be able to do work like this while we are on this amazing planet.

I saw the mother a few months later in the store. She shared how much they both appreciated the clearing that was done and that the daughter was doing really well working with the spirits and keeping the house clear.

September 2017: House and Spirit Clearing

Wow! This next clearing was a huge learning curve, not only for me but also for the person who was involved. About a year after writing my first book, I got a call from a person I had gotten to know, who would come into the place where I worked. He was frantic and looking for answers. He needed his place cleared as he was being energetically attacked at night.

When I got to the floor in the apartment building, as I was walking down the hallway to his unit, I could feel the heaviness of the energy. It felt thick, yucky and very unwelcoming. I shared this with him and let him know that yes, I did feel that something was wrong. Once I got in there, I lit the sage and started to smudge and do energy work for the apartment unit. It took quite a while before I could feel the difference. I also remember doing some energy work on him and cord-cutting to clear his field. There were a lot of attachments, but nothing that really stood out. I continued clearing and then got the sweetgrass going. The energy in the unit felt a lot better by the time I left. I felt like a person could relax in there again.

I got a call from this friend again, and he said that the attacks were still going on. I did another clearing for him at no charge, as this is my practice. I want the homeowner to be happy with the work I do. While smudging, I asked how these attacks were happening and what he felt. He shared that he would feel a wave of energy come over him, and it felt nasty. Then the cat would try to defend him and would sometimes almost bite him. The cat was trying to bite the spirit, not him. This fellow was losing hours of sleep with these attacks, and they had been going on for about two years and getting worse all the time. The cat was defending his human. When I left, I said to please let me know if this did not work.

When spirits are looking for help, they attach to someone who they believe can help them. If the person does not pay attention or is unaware of what is going on, the spirit's energy will become stronger and meaner over time. The spirit wants to go but it feels stuck on the earth plane.

A few days later, I was at the Calgary Body Soul & Spirit Expo sharing a booth with a dear friend. I got another call. He was really confused as there had been no change; he was still getting attacked and the cat finally did bite him. He ended up on a huge dose of antibiotics because of the cat bite. The next day he was leaving to B.C. for a few days. I asked him if he could come to the expo and I would try something totally different for him. He drove into the city for one more attempt.

I had the massage table at the expo and got him to lie down on it for an energy session. As I started with the Reiki, we were shown that all the work we had done to date with the clearings was meant to be, and the energies needed to be cleared to get to the root cause of the attacks. There had been a lot of heavy energy around this person for so long that the layers needed to be cleared with love and light first.

I asked my guide, Two Feathers, to show me what was going on and what we could do to help. What was shown to me was a little boy of about ten or 11. There was a long, curvy cord that went from this boy to the land where he was picked up. Following this cord,

I knew I was learning another lesson about spirit attachments and seeing deeper into the cause of a spirit's personal life. What I saw was a little boy who had been physically beaten. The child was born out of wedlock and abused by the biological father whom the mother was working for. The man's other son who was not born out of wedlock was treated well. As we sent healing energy to the child of the spirit in that lifetime, we were able to cut the cord to that life for him, too. What was magical and a huge surprise at the end was when Archangel Michael showed up. The little boy and Michael started to chat like old friends and walked away together. I breathed a huge sigh of relief and shared what I saw and heard. When I shared how the boy started to talk to Archangel Michael and that they both were excited to see each other again and chatting, my client smiled. He was really surprised at the outcome and understood when I shared that we needed to cut the cord for the spirit. Let the client know that he did the spirit a huge favour, yet it was unfortunate that it took him 2 years to find out what was going on.

A few months later, I was told a story about how my friend had gone to an old homestead where the spirit attached to him. There had been a bad fire on the land and the only building that did not burn was the homestead house. The day after the fire, the daughter showed up and asked if anyone had seen the ghost of a little boy who looked ragged. She shared that when her father was sick, this spirit showed up every day to visit the ailing man. I believe that this boy spirit may have been his brother or another male in the family blood line. There were a few people who had seen the spirit and were relieved to finally have someone speak to about him. This little boy finally found some peace and was able to get the chance to go to heaven.

This experience was a learning lesson for both of us. For me, it was the mediumship and seeing the life of the spirit, and also showing me the layers that a person needs to heal because of all the energy that is created after the spirit attaches to the client. For the client, it was learning that he, too, could help spirits cross over and learn to work with his guides and Archangel Michael.

Summer of 2018: Entity, Spirits and Land Clearing

I could not find this one in my journal, but I will never forget what I felt and saw during this house and land clearing. A young woman, the same age as one of my daughters got a hold of me. She was petrified to be in her house and there were so many things that were going wrong. The water was not running, one of her daughters was depressed, and the animals on the hobby farm were either getting hurt or going missing. She has three daughters, one of whom is strongly connected to the Fairy Realm. (I start sneezing when the fairies try to get my attention. Just sneezed three times as I was typing this.) The girls did not like going into the barn and would not go alone.

Since this clearing was a bit different from the others, I started with the barn. In the area where the small animals were being kept in large pens, there were two rooms. Both rooms were for holding supplies.

In the first room I saw a little girl of about nine or ten. She had curly blond hair and looked like she had been sick and died due to illness. She came from a time when there may have been little money in the family, and they could not afford to get her the help she needed. I sent this little girl a huge energy hug so that she could feel the love of the angels and God. When she shifted, I saw her walk away with an angel that was a nurse. Now this little one will get better on a soul level with heavens help. One of my friend's daughters saw the same girl spirit and it always freaked her out. She would not go to the barn alone. I was shown in a vision that the spirit latched on to the daughter when the girl was at her friend's place just down the road at another farm. The spirit knew that the daughter was a beautiful light being and could help the spirit get to where she really needed to be.

In the second room, on the right side of the door there were some saddles, reins and a strange portal that went from the roof to the floor. Most of the portals that I see are just on ground level. This was a dark portal and a dark figure was standing beside it. This was one time that I shook a bit and reminded myself that love is the strongest healing energy there is, and no one can get past me, the angels and elders. As a team, we all work together to heal spirit energy and the land. We sent out unconditional love. This room took awhile to clear. I had to put the smoking sage down and beam in the Reiki energy to shift the dark figure, then to close and seal in the portal.

On the west side of the building there was a huge riding arena; this was separate from the stables. As I went clockwise around the arena with the sage (being very careful with the embers of the sage so they did not drop into the straw), I talked to the landowner about life and what she and her girls were doing. I had not seen them in a long time. The arena was very well done and looked like a lot of love had been put into it. Suddenly, I got an overwhelming sense of sadness and loss. I asked if the previous owners had to sell at a huge loss. She shared that they did, something to do with an illness. Then I felt a lot of anger and asked about that. What happened is that the brother of the owner did the amazing work on the arena, and he did not get properly paid for the work that he did. For him, it represented a huge loss of time and dollars.

This all started to really make sense, as I said to my friend that the barn and land had a lot of potential. She saw the same thing; that is why she invested in the property. I told her not to give up and keep on seeing the vision she had in the first place.

Once we got the last owner's energy shifted back into positive energy for the barn, I picked up on another energy that would not let me go yet. As I was smudging, I noticed that I was not walking in the middle of the barn anymore. I put down the smudge bowl and placed my hands on the ground. I started to work with Blue. Blue is a blue energy force that works between the dimensions and helps on a multidimensional level. There are many things that I have forgotten about as a soul, and many energies that have been harmed during the thousands of years of Mother Earth's evolution. These are energies/spirits that get stuck and don't know where to go at the end of their existence. It took a while to heal the energies of the land and the arena. I just went with the flow and kept sending healing energy to the land.

Next, we headed toward the house. The house was where my friend did not want to be. The energy/lost spirit there tormented my friend. It played with lights and would not let her talk about it to friends. She was terrified.

As I went into the house, I did the same procedure as I would at any house: I started in the basement and headed to the top floor. If I remember correctly (I could not find this story in my journal although I swear I wrote it down), as I was smudging the basement, I could feel the energies down there, as my whole back was tensed up and it took a while to get down the stairs. I stayed in my heart centre and, of course, made sure the angels were with me. My friend was getting edgy, as she could feel the presence of the spirit that tormented her. She could see all the spirits heading to the far wall, where there was near a fireplace or a wall with a lot of bricks. When I do house clearings, while the sage is burning, I channel Reiki energy to dissolve any energy imprints in the house and to bring the love back to any lingering and lost spirits. As I got closer to the brick wall, the lost spirits slowly went with Archangel Michael. When the darker one left, my friend let me know that she felt him go. I felt a huge shift in my energy field and knew that the work in that area was done.

The rest of the house went easier. As I went into the bedrooms of the girls, information about each one of them came to me. I asked my friend about what I heard and got affirmations. The oldest girl, about 16, was very connected to the Fairy Realm and a lot more powerful than she realized. I gave her some suggestions to help work with her energy and the things that she picked up on each day. She was a strong empath and sometimes suffered from depression.

About a month later, I got a call to work on my friend's mom's home that was just down the same country road. Before she asked me to come out there, she shared that the water started to flow again in the taps at her house and that the animals out there were doing a lot better since the clearing we did.

There were two key areas in the mother's house that really got my attention and took extra time to clear. The first area was in the basement. There was a card table that was built to accommodate poker games. I know that when I was small, card games in the evening were an inexpensive way for the adults to have fun and enjoy some in-home entertainment. When I walked up to the table,

I felt the excessive drinking and unruly money gambling. Part of me thought that this was not right, but when I shared what I was feeling and seeing, again, I got the affirmations. The young adults who were playing poker had to finally quit the drinking and gambling when they realized the money it was costing and the effect on their health. Since then, the table saw no activity. We made sure the energy for that area was fully cleared before going on.

The second area of heavy energy was in a huge room where there used to be a swimming pool. The pool had been covered, and the room now held a billiard table. I think I spent about 20 minutes in this room. After 15 minutes, I asked Two Feathers what was going on. Then I was guided to ask the homeowner what was going on southwest of the property. She said that the land had been fracked several months before for oil extraction. Fracking of the land is dangerous, and the chemicals being pushed into the land are very toxic. From this, I knew again that we needed to concentrate on working with Blue to heal the lost energies and clear the land of the imprints and the energy that travelled from the fracking. After another five minutes, I was able to leave the room. Later, I remembered doing the same at my friend's place but had not connected it to the fracking.

Winter 2019: Land and Lost Soul Clearing

I think it was around February of 2019 when I was called into the city to do a clearing. The client had felt a nasty energy that bothered her at night. The spirit was getting meaner.

The first room that we came to, was the family room in the basement. The only time the client and her boyfriend would go in there was to watch *Game of Thrones*. That was the only time they would come into this room. As I stood in front of the couch, I could picture a young couple and a child buried underneath the house. So as not to startle the client, I wondered out loud what had happened on the land before the new house was built. We never know where gravesites might be. She shared how the builder had mentioned that if he were to find something, he would not say a word, as it could hold up the construction for months and tie up the dollars that were invested in the project. This statement from her answered what I wanted to share. I told her that I saw the bodies, but that the energy was cleared for the humans that were buried there and not to worry. No matter where we go there is the possibility of finding bones of some sort on the land.

Her kitchen held a surprise for me, too, and not a giddy one. When I got to the main floor, the dining area and entranceway was smudged, the energy not too bad. When I arrived at the kitchen, I got an eerie feeling. I poured out the love and light. Suddenly, a hand came out to grab mine, and it was a mean, nasty feeling. This hand came from a child about four feet tall. I can still remember how startled I was and a wee bit scared. I was also mad that the spirit would try to hurt me; this was so unacceptable. I don't take this work lightly and know that we need to be careful, yet this was the first time something tried to lash out at me. As this child spirit was beamed with love and light, I slowly quit shaking and knew that the spirit would get the help that it needed. Finally, I saw the little one leave. I can't remember if it was bagged in white netting or taken by two angels.

The next room held another surprise and not a pleasant one either. In my mind's eye, I saw the bones of several babies. These bones were either from babies who did not survive their birth or were aborted as the mother could not look after them. This was a LONG time ago, in the south-west part of Calgary. The location made sense and the events that happened made sense, too. This was from a time when there was no hospital or support for unwed mothers. What I felt was the sadness due to the loss of the littles ones. I wonder what the owners of the land from that time period went through. They must have felt they had no other option for the burial. I sent lots of love and light to the land and the little ones.

June 17, 2019: House and Human Clearing

I got a call to come back to a friend's house to do another clearing. The friend mentioned that the last week had been hard for her, energetically, and that nothing was going right. She had done her best to smudge and clear the house, but nothing was working.

As I drove up to the house, I could feel the fairy energy. The fairies were not very happy. After I stepped inside, my friend's sister mentioned that the lights at the doorway flickered just as I drove up to the house. Everyone there saw it happen. Right away, the sister said: "Kim is here. Something here is pissed off." I giggled when I heard this. When I go to do clearings, I bring the angels and the ancestors to work with me and for their support, an awesome team

As I was getting the sage and sweetgrass ready for the clearing, I asked what was going on. As my friend was chatting, my mind went to one of her daughters who was not there at the time. She was at work. I asked if her daughter was depressed and having a hard time. She said yes. I asked if we could do a clearing for her, as my friend could be a surrogate for her daughter and give me permission to do so. I checked into the daughter's energy field and saw when the chaos started, shared this, and got another yes from the mom. I started to do energy work to shift the energy of the spirit that was attached to the girl. This took quite a while, as the energy was dark. That is why the lights flickered when I got there; the spirit was reluctant to go. After a while, the spirit was taken by Archangel Michael to the other side for help.

Once I got the daughter cleared, we started the house clearing. I remember getting stuck on the stairs. I had to sit down for a bit and send lots of love and light healing energy into the basement so that I could energetically go down there. When I have the sage going, it feels like I have really strong Spidey senses. The spirit that was attached to the daughter had left a heavy imprint in the basement. Once the energy shifted, I went down the rest of the stairs and into the first room where the freezer was. As soon as the room got cleared, I giggled. I could hear the fairies say that they could leave booby traps again. I asked the youngest daughter if fairies could really set booby traps and she said yes! This amazing young woman is very connected to the Fairy Realm, it was a joy to get her affirmation.

The last room in the basement was the oldest daughter's room who had the spirit attachment. As I smudged the room, all the girls gathered in there and sat on the bed or stood along the wall. It was quite interesting, as this had not happened in any other home. The girls started to talk about a cousin who had passed away.

After asking a few guided questions, I had a strong feeling that this cousin of the girls was a strong empath and had no one to talk to. She became mean and reclusive and would not join the other cousins at family gatherings. When we started to talk about the cousin who had passed away, the light in the room flickered. We all knew that the cousin was there.

After a lengthy discussion, the girls asked the cousin (in spirit, on the other side) to help them with doing healing work on this planet. They said they would ask her for support when they needed it. This talk was a healing experience, not only for the cousin but for all the girls in the room.

The rest of the house was easy to clear. After the sage, we went through with the sweetgrass. At the end, the fairies that lived on the land, the family and the home were all happy again.

February 1, 2019: House and Entity/Spirit Clearing

This house was interesting, as there were a few things going on in there energetically. Before I started, the client shared that the home had been rented out for a year while they travelled.

I always start the clearing in the basement. As I went through the basement, the energy I was picking up on was from the renters. There were several spots where I believe fights or arguments had taken place. Some of the male's anger (homeowner) showed up along a wall where there were some repairs that had been done in the past. This kind of energy can leave imprints and make it uncomfortable for those who are energy sensitive. Throughout the rest of the house, again, the energy of the tenants kept showing up.

In the child's room, I had a hard time clearing the energy. It felt like something was bothering the little one. The mother shared that the child was having a hard time sleeping. I was sure that the room was cleared and told the mother to call me if the child continued having bad dreams.

The next evening, I got a call: the little one had another rough night. I checked into the little guy's energy field. This spirit was somehow connected to another family member too. While doing the clearing, we needed to send love and light along a cord to heal the connection for both the child and whoever the spirit had attached to in the first place. It's interesting how sometimes we need to reconnect again after the initial clearing. Sort of like letting the dust settle to see what is still lingering.

February 1, 2019: Spirit Clearing

For this story I will call the male homeowner, Fred, and his friend, Harry.

In this house, I found a spirit in the master bath. The sense I got was that this spirit, Harry, was jealous of Fred, who lived in the house. This spirit did not want Fred to succeed in life. After I was able to help the spirit of Harry to cross over to the other side, I shared the story with Fred's wife. She said that her husband did not like using the bathroom in the master bedroom and the same thing happened in the last house that they had lived in. He always wanted the bathroom door to be closed.

Several years before, a good friend of his committed suicide. This friend, Harry, suffered from depression and had always held a poor-me attitude. He seemed to be envious of how things went for Fred, whether it be work or relationships. After Harry took his life, he clung onto Fred and followed him to each place that he moved to.

Sometimes we never find out where these feelings come from, and people have a hard time living in that state of well-being. Especially when they do not know that answers and solutions can be found to heal them. We can heal energetically and find out where our depression or thought patterns come from. We can release the thought patterns and create new ones. Hopefully the spirit that we released will find a sense of peace in its next lifetime.

March 5, 2019: Mediumship and Lost Fairy Spirit

I love it when we get to see things, whether in the third eye or in the mind's eye. How many hundreds of people have told their children that the things they see are something that they made up, that they are just telling stories, when in reality, what we see in our mind's eye is real, as we are sensing the energy of other existences from other dimensions. This is what I see in the house clearings, and this one was no exception.

I was called to do a clearing in a house in a beautiful community in far south-west Calgary. As I was smudging the house, it felt like everything seemed calm and peaceful there. When we got to the kitchen, I can't remember what I felt, but I started to ask the lady about her dad. When I shared with her how much he loved and cherished her, I could feel his love, and tears of joy were running down my cheeks. She was so grateful to hear this as he was no longer here. He apologized about the absence of the love she needed. When this lady was growing up, her mother was unwell and needed to be in a nursing home. Unable to visit her mother, this client grew up not being able to experience motherly love. Yet she was an amazing mother and provided her children with support every day and they truly cherish her. She is an incredible mom and wife.

After clearing the kitchen, we went to the bedrooms of her daughters. I could feel the energy of the girls in the rooms and offered suggestions for each girl to help them out in school and with work. The girls are energetically sensitive like their mom.

The last room in the house was a surprise. I could feel something as soon as I stepped inside the door and I mentioned this to the homeowner. She said that one of her daughters did not like this room, and there were problems with water leaking in there. At the far end of the room, there was a little closet. When I opened the door, I could see something in the corner, bunched up in a ball. As I beamed in love and light, I could feel the energy change. The bundle in the corner slowly stood up. There was a fairy with long dark hair and huge eyes looking at me. I saw the smile, heard a thank you, and then she was gone. That was the second time I saw a fairy stuck and unable to move from a location. What brought her there? Was she lost? Did she get left behind? Was it a human who took advantage of her and cornered her in the closet? This had happened before the present family moved in. The fairy is now free and back with her kinfolk.

July 9, 2019: Two Lost Spirits, a Drug Dealer, the Other Died from an Overdose

I have a dear friend, Joe, who sees spirits, and he has gotten a lot of affirmations and signs from them—from seeing imprints on his bed from his grandmother lying on it, to getting major goosebumps on his arms when coming home to find dirt on his floor that should not have been there.

On this day, he called and said he could not be in the house. There was dirt on the floor, and there were noises downstairs along the back wall. It sounded like planks of wood were banging together. He had goosebumps on his arm that he took a picture of. He was scared. I brought my friend with me and made sure that we were safe to travel there. On the way, we both picked up on an older gentleman spirit. As soon as I went into the house (both my friends stayed outside for a few minutes), I could feel the heavy energy. I went into the kitchen to get the sage going and started going into energy mode. By the time I was ready, the fellows had caught up. I started to take the stairs down to the basement, and I saw that the portal at the back door needed to be closed. After closing the portal, I found out that a woman had let Joe know that the portal was there and that is why he got a lot of activity at his place. When portals are open, not everything that comes through is nice.

As I slowly made my way down the stairs, I had to stop every second step to change the energy. I could feel it all the way down my back. When I reached the basement, my stomach got queasy. Right away, I knew that there were two spirits down there. One on the north side of the building, and the other on the south side by the fake Christmas tree. The one on the north side was the older man that we saw on the way to Joe's place. I got an image of needle tracks all the way down his arms and the sense that he had died from an overdose. This was why I was feeling sick to my stomach. The chemicals and decaying of his human body that occurred while he was taking the drugs must have been a horrid way to live each day. I brought in the energy this spirit needed to help him shift and go to heaven.

Next, I went to the south side of the building, which was out of sync for me as it was not clockwise. What I saw was the drug dealer, and I wondered if both men had died at the same time. I asked out loud what would make a person turn to a drug dealer? The energy of the spirit turned from an adult to a ten-year-old boy and he pointed out the Christmas tree. Did he want money as a child for his family for Christmas? Selling drugs was his answer as a child to bring in income. As we shifted the energy, my stomach started to feel better and so did both of my friends' stomach. They both got the same sick feeling when they came downstairs. Once the little boy spirit went over to the other side, we were all able to relax.

After I got home, I got a call from Joe. He had gone outside then went back in to sweep up the dirt on the floor. The dirt was all gone.

August 13, 2019: House Clearing to Release Past Owners

I got a call from a client who'd moved into a home that had previous owners. I had done a clearing for this woman's daughter a few months ago. The reason why I am sharing this one is that most of the family members did not like the energies in the house and each of them picked up on something different.

When I got up the next morning, I still felt sleepy. I knew that the place I was living in needed a clearing after going to the client's place. While driving to the house for the clearing, I did some energy work to try to clear my space, to reduce the drowsy feeling. I wondered if the feeling was from the client's home or mine.

As soon as I got there, she let me know that there were stain marks on the carpet in the basement. The dogs would go down there to be peeing in that one spot. Once the sage was ready, I headed for the basement and stopped before I even got to the stairs. After a bit, I went down, but I was feeling deep sadness and depression. It felt like the previous male owner was in the family room and needed to be energetically disconnected from the house. She then shared that the house was sold because of a divorce. I got a sense that the male spent most of his time hiding down there from his wife. I wonder if the dogs were trying to cover the anger of the male that had been there by peeing on the same spot and wanted the male energy to leave.

I went upstairs and got a very heavy feeling in the kitchen. I shared how the kitchen was the heart of the family. The present owner told me that she heard that the previous female owner, the wife of the fellow who lived in the basement, was not easy to work with. Mean and controlling. No compassion for others. Stubborn. Unhappy. It took a while to clear the kitchen, and I also did a cord-cutting for the unhappy lady.

While in the kitchen, I started to think of the garage and knew it needed to be cleared. It felt like there was a lot of anger in there. Were there actual fist fights that happened in the garage? As I started on the garage, the client told me that her daughter had said the energy in there felt like a grandmother's energy, the client's grandmother who had passed away. This grandmother was angry, belittling, yelled a lot and never seemed happy. I did a cord-cutting for the client and her grandmother while working on the garage. I explained that many times, we have no idea why our older family members are the way they are, and to let go with unconditional love.

In conclusion:

What I have loved about all of this—the spirit clearings and healing the imprints left behind—is the change that the clearings have made for the families and their homes. From family members feeling depression, anxiety, being scared to death, and experiencing other uncomfortable feelings, to becoming comfortable and feeling the joy and love come back into their home, is magical. To know that we can energetically bring the love and light back in brings a sense of relief and the promise of hope. Being in the heart centre, being able to connect with the energetic field of home and lands is magical. Being able to help lost souls return to the light is an amazing honour to be able to provide.

CHAPTER 4

Working with the Animal Kingdom

I find animals fun to watch. I often stop to talk to birds, especially crows. When I see animals, I wonder what is going through their minds. Are they able to enjoy life unbothered by crazy thoughts? Are they creatures that can really enjoy life? Do they see the foliage the way I do? Beautiful, vibrant, and magical?

We had a dog named Romeo. I truly believe that he still comes to visit me in dream time and sometimes is with me on the walks that I take. A psychic once told me that Romeo was my camel in another life. He brought so much joy to all of us. I know that he could see spirits. One day when I asked him why he barked at them, he gave me this look as if to say, why not? He knew exactly what I was talking about. Romeo had a special place in everyone's heart and the only one that he challenged was my granddaughter. He wanted to be the only child and was a wee bit pissed that he had to share the spotlight.

Over the years, after I got interested in wholistic healing, both my oldest daughter and granddaughter would buy me gifts that were wolf themed. I always wondered why they were giving me wolves and where this was coming from. I really did love the presents. Later, when talking to a shaman, he let me know that my two totem animals were the wolf and the fox. This was the affirmation that I had been looking for.

Around 2005, I was attending a workshop and there was a young woman there who shared messages about totem animals that she saw with people. I became curious about this. I asked my spirit guide to help me see them around my friends and clients. Over time, the animals would appear during treatments and sometimes when just talking to someone. Once in a blue moon, I would want to share this information with a total stranger and needed to get over the fear that they would think I was crazy. I felt this information was being shared with me for a reason.

I started to share totem animal information in newsletters that I posted, and along the way I realized that my guide had more to share with me. When I see a totem animal, it appears on the left side of a person. Sometimes there are two of them. If I see an animal spirit on the right side of a person, this animal spirit is there for a specific amount of time to help the person through a transition. There have been many times that I've shared this information and the person has been very grateful. They read the message from the animal and they get a huge affirmation that they have been looking for.

For myself, the wolf and fox have been very important messages for me, as I've realized that this is the kind of life that I am living. A few years ago, a good friend pointed out a fox that we had both seen on the way home from an event. She shared that the fox was there as a message for me. This was before talking to the shaman.

$$* \quad * \quad *$$

The fox represents camouflage, as the fox can blend into its natural environment. He can sit in the background and just observe while others are involved in their own activities. During the wintertime, the fur of the fox turns white to blend in with the snow, and in the summer, it turns a reddish brown.

The fox also provides protection for the family unit. He/she watches over the family and makes sure that no one comes into danger. Whether the family is stationary or travelling, the fox is aware of everything that is going on and his actions are undetected. Fast, quick-thinking and sure-footed, the fox is ready to step in and help at any time.

Fox medicine can teach us to observe and watch, rather than get involved. One can learn to bounce from situation to situation, knowing just what is needed for that moment; to shapeshift in order to fit into one's environment, or even to anticipate what will happen next. One can learn to observe and know what is going on without hearing any words being spoken. One can learn to be somewhere without being noticed.

The fox also teaches us how we can use many methods of healing: the animal kingdom, angels, God, crystals, and herbs. Whatever is needed for that person or situation. It teaches us how we can create the healthy world and life that our bodies need. The fox can travel to the other realms. It knows the magic of connecting to the Fairy Realm and has supernatural power. If the fox has come to you, it may be time to get connected with the Fairy Realm and all that they can teach you. This is the time to become more in tune with your psychic abilities. Foxes also represent femininity and will show even the males that they need to be in touch with both their male and female energies.

*　　*　　*

Finally, the fox represents cunning (anticipating the next move), and can mean that maybe you are being foolish, and not being who you truly are. The fox will show up when we try to stand out too much. Why are we trying to draw attention to ourselves? The fox is the one that stands aside, unobserved, but can be called upon when needed. The fox does not draw attention to itself.

The wolf is the teacher and represents loyalty, guardianship and spirit.

When the wolf comes into our lives, we are shown that we are protected, and that we are part of our community. The wolf allows us to teach the medicines of the land for a healthier community. He is known to teach children about respect, and lessons for growth and living a humble existence.

Sirius is known as the Dog Star, which is represented by the wolf in Africa, Egypt and America. The wolf's loyalty brings us back to our home and origins: to look after the community and bring people together for growth and lessons. The wolf is known to be the greatest teacher.

The moon and the wolf are connected; both tap into the wisdom and psychic energies that we can all be a part of. When the moon is full, the energy is very strong and attracts both wolf and man to seek deeper wisdom. There are times when we need to be alone to receive our greatest lessons. This is the time to reflect and absorb experiences and allow ourselves to immerse ourselves in our inner wisdom and bring back old memories of the ancient ones.

The wolf is not a fighter but will let you know when you have overstepped boundaries. You will get a growl first, to let you know that your behaviour is not acceptable. When you work with this wise teacher, you learn that when you truly embrace your gifts, you can be proud of who you are, and you don't have to prove anything to others.

Within the community, wolves are taught at a young age how to be aware of others and their own reactions. How to watch body language and listen carefully to the voice. What is the person really saying? Wolf lessons also share how to effectively govern a group, how to keep the balance and how inner discipline brings real freedom. The wolf's senses of smell, knowing and sight are very strong, and this can help to pick up on dangers and those who do not travel in the heart centre.

The crow/raven and wolf are said to work together. They will lead each other to food. Those with a wolf totem are also working with the raven.

$$*\quad*\quad*$$

After learning about the animal totems above, stories came flooding into my mind. In a present friendship with someone that is close to me, the fox has come forward a few times, and when we read up on it, we realized the tie I had to both the fox and the Fairy Realm. One should not take advantage of a person who is so connected to the Fairy Realm, as the truth will always be known. The energies of both the fox and the Fairy Realm can be intense and very protective.

As for the wolf, I know he travels with me, and I have a story about this from one of my trips to Australia, which I will share later. Having worked with the wolf for a few years and talking to crows/ravens, I finally figured out the connection in 2018. While a good friend was doing energy work on me, she found out that my spirit guide's, Two Feathers', totem animal is the crow. This helped me to understand why I was getting so many strong messages from crows: Two Feathers, my guide, was speaking to me.

My Introduction to Spirit Animals in Spirit Form

In a house that I lived in for several years, my daughters and I all felt the presence of a small dog that used to live there. This dog would jump up on the bed at night. We all just accepted it, and none of us ever got nervous.

My first visit to Australia in 2010 was when the animals started to talk to me, then they would come to visit me during dream time.

November 2010

Before I went to Australia in 2010, my body was shifting energetically and there were times when I could feel the adrenaline going wild in my legs. I was nervous and scared yet extremely excited, as I was going to go visit my dad's homeland. A dear friend said that my body was getting ready for the changes that were coming. As I was boarding the plane, I asked my friend Dragon to fly with me as I was petrified of the long flight ahead, and of being that far away from my daughters for the first time and being over the ocean for so many hours.

Once I arrived in Australia, I began undertaking a new journey on a spiritual basis. This started slowly at first, then got stronger as the days went by. I could feel the energy of the earth run up my legs; it felt like my legs were encased in balloons. My feet felt tingly and the animals were responding to me in magical ways. The energy of the earth is as old as the dragons, and going to Australia, I was going home, even though in this lifetime I had not been there before.

At my auntie's in Sydney, little birds were landing and walking up my legs. What an honour! She was not impressed but I sure was. In the Bunya Mountains, north-west of Brisbane, I started talking to a wallaby that was wandering around. A wallaby is a small kangaroo and they can be friendlier than kangaroos. I saw the wallaby by the outhouse and started to talk to her. I asked, "What is that little one? What is in front of you?" She looked at me and watched. Then it dawned on me and I asked, "It that a baby that you have? Can I please see your little one?" My soft voice had her attention and she much have felt safe, as she slowly turned around to show me the little one in her pouch. She stood there for a while so that I could get a good look and I was able to show my cousin. I was honoured to be acknowledged by the mother wallaby. My spiritual journey continued as I went to stay with different relatives, and I could feel the spirit energy of the animals at nighttime, too.

The most magical animal experience I had there was when my uncle took me to the beach where my dad's ashes were scattered. Once we got to the beach, I needed to use the washroom and told my uncle that I would meet him at the top of the hill. After getting out of the washroom, I saw an Australian dog standing by my uncle and asked who his friend was. He had no idea where the dog came from and was surprised that the dog took a liking to him. I went down to the beach to say goodbye to my dad, as I was not able to be there when the ashes were scattered. The dog followed me down and brought a stick over to me. When I went to reach for the stick, he growled. Being cautious, I told the dog that I would play with him later, then I walked over to the ocean and into the water. It felt so good to be there. I talked to Dad for a bit and told him how much I loved him and how much he was missed. I knew Dad was okay and that his spirit was in heaven, and I felt at peace.

After a bit of time, I turned around, walked out of the water, and went to get the stick to throw for the dog. I felt as if he was waiting for me to be done. When I was getting ready to throw the stick for the third time, knowing I needed to get back to my uncle, I told the dog that this was to be the last throw. I walked back to the stairs and seeing my uncle's eyes, I knew that he missed my dad a great deal, too. At the same time, we both looked toward the dog that had befriended him and had let me throw the stick for him. We saw the dog trying to bury the stick. We both knew that the dog was there for my dad and that Dad was thanking us both for showing up and saying goodbye. Huge gratitude again for the animal kingdom speaking to both of us.

December 2010, and Onward

The Kitten

After I got home, the animal spirits started to show up at nighttime, as I was trying to get to sleep. The first time I was lying in bed facing the wall. I was on the edge of the mattress and heard a wee *meow* and the sound of something climbing up the mattress of the bed. I lay there quiet and still, as I so wanted to be able to hear and feel the spirits more. The little spirit kitten walked across the back of my head. With my eyes still closed, trying to be still and not scared, I could feel the kitten tickle my face with its fur. It then settled down beside me, and I fell right asleep. For me, spirit energy is strong and can pull me into sleep very quickly.

The Lynx

Shortly after this visit, the kitten came into my room a couple more times, and then I felt a lynx crawl up on my stomach. This one was another shock, as the spirit energy slowly eased up on my stomach, as I lay in bed. I was nervous. Yet, again, I so wanted to feel the spirit energy and connect with the animal kingdom.

The lynx message was telling me to acknowledge my own gifts and talents. My clairvoyance and clairaudience skills were getting stronger.

Clairvoyance - to see visions; vivid dreams; to see or hear something several times; to see lights and sparkles; to dream of lost ones.

Clairaudience – to hear audible messages, whether through sound, music or noises; to hear someone call your name or hear a deceased relative or angel talking to you.

As I was doing more work with clients and helping them to learn more about what they were capable of doing in life, this message from the lynx showed me that I was on the right track and to always support others in their growth.

The Hawk

This visit scared me, yet I knew that I really needed to listen and be still. Not to back down or allow any fears to come in.

I was lying on my back in my bed at night when I felt the talons of a bird grip onto the toes of my feet. I could really feel the pressure, and it was a bit uncomfortable, but I stayed still until I fell asleep after I thanked the hawk for being there with me.

When I read about the hawk the next morning, it all made sense. I was going through a huge transformation, and it was magical.

The hawk is also like the raven; they are messengers for us. When I see the hawk, I am reminded to remember to trust and know that all is well. The hawk, especially the red-tailed hawk, is a symbol of working with the Kundalini (energy), which starts at the base of the spine. Once the Kundalini is fully open, one is more prepared to pursue one's life purpose and their childhood dreams come to fruition. (I remember pretending to save people when I was about eight years old. I would get lost in the daydreams about how I would do this.) The Kundalini brings harmony and higher levels of consciousness, including the heightening of psychic abilities. The hawk is also associated with the 14th card of the Tarot deck. This card is the Temperance card, a symbol of vision and being able to do astral travel.

A Visit from a Huge Group of Animal Spirits

Wow! The last impressive visit during that time, I got from the animal spirits at night, was a visit from so many animal spirits that I lost count of who was there. There were birds, the kitten, a huge bear (thankfully, he stayed on the floor beside the bed), the wolf and the lynx. All the spirits slowly settled in on top of me and beside me, and I was both honoured and confused as to why there were so many that night.

As I got more comfortable, I was able to see who was on me and where they were located. I started to drift off a few minutes later, but then there was a loud noise in the living room. Suddenly, the animal spirits got up and went running down the hallway. I could hear the rush of them all running and flying, and it seemed as if they were there to protect me and make sure that whatever was in the living room got nowhere near me. I thanked all of them, even though I was still in shock over what I had witnessed. To this day, I will never forget this event and how powerful our wonderful friends from the animal kingdom are.

Spirit Animals as Guides

It was so much fun learning how to pick up on clients' spirit helpers and being able to share who was with them. Healers see the spirits and their purpose differently. What I was being taught by my spirit guide came close to what the shaman saw and shared. When I see an animal spirit on the left side of someone, the spirit appears to be with the human for their lifetime. When the animal spirit shows up on the right side, the spirit is here to help them to learn or to help during a transition that they are about to go through in their life.

More Transformations in 2018 and Connections to Animal Spirits

March 11, 2018 (Petrie, Australia)

One night, I had a vivid dream where I was helping a good friend with an event. We were cleaning up, even picking up cigarette butts. My friend was anticipating a reward for the work she'd done and looking after Mother Earth at the same time. I saw a truck with giant paintings in the back. I was talking out loud and sharing with someone else how hard Anita had worked for this event and that I hoped she would be rewarded for her efforts. Suddenly, in front of me stood a very handsome Native American fellow, younger than I, with long dark hair. He was the one who was to gift Anita with a painting. I gave him a huge hug and said thank you. He said, "I know you," to which I replied, "Yes, I remember you, too. We have met in many lives." He nodded yes.

Woke up in the morning and looked outside to see both a crow and a magpie outside. I believe I saw the crow that morning because my spirit guide, Two Feathers, is a Native American medicine man, and I had recently been told that his totem animal is the crow. The crow was bringing me another message.

The crow signifies that one is on the verge of manifesting something big. (This sighting was just before realizing that I was to anchor in my third book and knowing that it would be while in Australia.)

The magpie tells us that we should act on all opportunities that present themselves and be clear with our communication.

The following night, I dreamed about a spider. This is something that I had dreamed of a few times, and the dreams had mainly focused on the spider's web. I took this to mean that stories from my dreams and experiences were being woven together, recorded in my journals, to show me that I was working with so many dimensions

The spider was telling me to write creatively without limits, and to be inspired by nature. This message reminded me of the pictures that I draw of animals and plants, the beauty of nature, and how it influences our lives.

That morning I started to think of the phoenix energy that was north of Toowoomba. There was a street called Phoenix Way that my cousins lived by. Before I had gone back to Petrie, after the

Wellness Expo in Brisbane, I travelled south-west in Queensland to visit family there.

The phoenix teaches us about transformation; rebirth.

During my week in Toowoomba, the birds were talking loudly to me each day. This was where I began to work with my new Dragonfae cards', and my cousins helped me to feel more relaxed after the expo. This was also the place that I got three sets of mysterious double-fanged snakebites on my lower legs. Where we had walked that evening, there was no way that I could have been bitten by a snake without knowing. I had to put some tea tree oil on the marks to take the sting out of the punctures. Still wondering how this could happen and the significance of the phantom bites.

The snake represents rebirth: the shedding of old ways, transformation and healing. Resurrection and initiation: to grow into a newer state of well-being. Wisdom: to use what we have learned and implement the teaching in our lives. The snake also plays a role in guarding sacred places, such as the role of the serpent and the dragon.

The dragon represents entering a new phase of life and reminds us to keep our connection to past lives that held Earth-based spiritual practices: the shamans, the medicine women, the dragon keepers. We are reminded that we are always protected on these new journeys.

March 16, 2018

Getting ready to sit down with my morning coffee on the deck in Petrie, I was looking around at the outdoor plants. I spotted something green on one of the plants, a shade different than the rest of the leaf and with a spot of red. As I looked closer, I realized it was a translucent-looking grasshopper. You could see where he was eating the leaves of the plant.

Grasshoppers represent taking a leap of faith and listening to our inner voice. They symbolize good news coming in and rapid change.

In Petrie, each evening, my friend and I sat outside listening to the night animals, talking and sharing stories about our experiences as healers and energy workers. We shared how the animals and universe talk to us, especially when we finally slow down long enough to listen. We can learn so many earth lessons from them and start to understand what it is required from us to move forward in life.

Travelling with My Animal Spirit Team

As I travel, I ask both the angels and the animal kingdom to be with me. My dragon friend on the roof of my car, the wolf and fox, either inside the car or running alongside it. There were a few times, in 2016, while driving in Australia that I was reminded that they were there with me. I would stop the car and open the back hatch. Right away, I could feel either the wolf or the fox jumped out the back. There were a couple of times when I could see their energy go flying out. I made sure to thank them each time.

CHAPTER 5

Working with the Angels
and Ascended Masters

As we travel from our root chakra to our crown chakra, we are learning how to be connected to Mother Earth and survive in the human bodies that we were given. We also learn how to connect again with the heavens and other galaxies, as our true memories come back into existence.

Angels

In 2002, I was introduced to the Angelic Realm. Even though I knew I had a guardian angel, I did not realize how much work the angels did for us. A few years ago, I was having a bad dream, and my daughter heard me crying out and asking my dad where my angel was. He must have told us about angels when we were little kids. Over the last few years, I've come to learn just how much we all work together.

I have read articles that talk about how angelic beings can be seen and can appear in pictures, and people would share how they could hear the singing of the angels in churches. Many people have reported seeing angels around them. I believe that they truly are there but in a translucent state. You can see them but not in a solid state, as we would see a human. We can also feel the presence of angels by their energy, or even by a touch.

You may have heard that some angels are fallen angels. Some religious groups do not believe in angels. Someone tried telling me a few years ago that angels were not needed anymore. Right away, without thinking about it, I blurted out, "Yes, they are needed and will be around for a long time." A psychic who was with us shared that she heard the angels say thank you for saying this.

There are pictures and murals that were painted a long time ago depicting angels and cherubs showing their love and compassion for humankind. There are stories about angels being present during trying times. Angels have appeared as humans and disappeared into the ether as fast as they appeared. Apparitions of angels have been seen in rooms during a sickness of a family member or while waiting for someone to pass on from a lengthy illness.

Archangel Michael was the first angel I heard about. For some unknown reason, I felt uneasy, wondering why this angel was called an archangel. Was this angel good? Then I heard about Archangel Raphael. I saw the energy of this angel beside an instructor during a class. The angel had a green energy and seemed about the same height as the instructor and was standing at her right side. Another student saw the same thing during the class! In this workshop, I learned more about the angels and the role they play in heaven and on earth. At first, I did not work with the angels all that much, but after hearing a lot more about them, they started to become a big part of the healing work and house clearings I do.

My first experience working with Archangel Michael was after I learned why I was having a tough time while driving my car from Calgary to Cochrane (Alberta, Canada). A fellow practitioner said to say the following the next time I travel the road: "Archangel Michael, please be with me: to the left of me, to the right of me, in front of me, behind me, above me and below me." This is what I did the next time I was driving back from Calgary. As soon as I got about 500 metres from Glendale road, it felt like I had entered a vortex of energy. It was a strange feeling. As mentioned in *The Essence of Who We Are*, I found out that this part of the highway was known for having a lot of car accidents. This gathering of spirits was why I was having a tough time and kept on wanting to fall asleep at the wheel. Once we helped the spirits to cross over, I have not, since then, felt the same sleepy energy there.

Since this, Archangel Michael has helped me with house clearings and provided protection during the clearings. He and his team help the spirits, no matter how lost they are, and no matter what they have done in their lifetime, to go to heaven. From what I understand, the reluctant spirits are taken for what we call "further processing." Some may need some help before they proceed to get a review of their life or lives before continuing to another life.

This was the start of my relationship with Archangel Michael. Shortly after this, I started to do house clearings and have always asked Archangel Michael to contain the lost spirits until I get to the house to do the full clearing. No matter how heavy the energy of the lost spirit (a client may consider it "evil" or "demon-like"), I see them as being lost. Some of them get tired of being stuck here and don't know how to cross over. Some are nasty and angry and don't care. With unconditional love and compassion from a human and the protection and support of the angels, all the spirits can make the transition.

God/Creator exists within each one of us and can be found around us in all the living forms. It was not until my early 40s, that I truly started to understand that angels are real. Angels, archangels, cherubs and other heavenly beings do exist. I first needed to be reminded that God/Creator is real, and I now know that we do have angels here to help us when we ask.

The Angelic Realm

Heaven's Angels

Angels go through training where they learn about unconditional love and being at peace with God and the universe. We have angels that work in the heavens and outer realms. Angels that work beside God and Brother Jesus, work on the other side to help those in need there and on planet Earth. These heavenly angels are in spirit form and can communicate with us, and their presence is felt in several ways.

These angels we can only see in spirit form. I personally feel the angels and know when they are around and will be very grateful when I can see them again. One of the children that I looked after used to be able to see them when she was little. She let me know when the angels were around me to help. The heavenly angels help us out when they are called upon. You must ask aloud for their help so that they can hear you. They can not hear us as well if we just ask silently. They all have different roles and responsibilities.

Guardian Angels

When I was sitting in the backyard, I had a memory of asking for this amazing home and the gardens for the girls to play in, and I realized that I had been truly talking to God, my angels and the universe. They all heard me and helped to bring this dream to fruition. My heart expanded and I felt the strength of the love that the universe had for me and knew that my guardian angel had my back. I remember many nights as I was growing up, where I would ask my angels to guard me and help to take away my bad dreams and help me find peace and love within. This always gave me a peaceful feeling so that I could get back to sleep again.

Maybe three to four years later, after having this realization about God, a dear friend shared during an energy session that I had a guardian angel who was sitting in the corner of the room watching over me. Again, I was tickled pink to think that I was worthy of having such support and that someone else saw this beautiful angelic being. It was amazing to know that someone else acknowledged the angels and believed in them.

Please remember that I do not attend church, have little religious training and walked away from the church when they insisted that I must memorize things from the Bible and another book for me to be confirmed in the Anglican Church. It felt so wrong that one needed to memorize words that were not in current English. Why would God make us do such things? This seemed to me very robotic, and not representative of real love for the God who we were to believe in. Even though I proclaimed to be atheist for many years, I still had the sense that there was something more in the universe.

Earth Angels

Some angels have specific missions and are trained to help families get through crises and assist with the evolution of souls that are finding it tough to evolve. This may be part of their training or something that they agreed to help with, like a community service. These angels will come to earth to help teach humans lessons and bring awareness about spirituality and about the true essence of who we are. Like humans, these angels sometimes go through tough times to be able to share their experiences as learning tools and strong messages to the world.

A family of five may have one angel in their home as either a parent or a child. This person will be the one who will help the family learn their lessons, be the support person that they need and bring love and compassion back to the family. This earth angel is helping individuals learn and see that there are other options to what they have experienced in other lifetimes. Some of the families will awaken or evolve, and some will have one to two members who understand the empathic and angelic lessons that will help them move forward and break the chain of unhealthy thinking that has been passed down through generations.

These angels are known as earth angels. Many of these angels are unaware of who they are and when they find out, they stay humble and genuine. Their stories are shared with love and compassion; they learn quickly how ego can be both healthy and unhealthy. Their faith is very strong, and they don't seem to give up. They can also feel sadness, anger, frustration and all the other human emotions. Many earth angels have a hard time here, as the energies and the understanding of true love on the earth plane is different than in the angelic realm. The energy here on earth is heavier, due to the chaos that Mother Earth has felt over the thousands of years it has been ruled by humans. Many earth angels are empathic, and their intuition is strong.

Angels are here to protect us.

Once, when I was driving in a nasty winter storm, coming down a hill into town, I felt scared to death. This secondary highway is always poorly maintained during storms, and the poor visibility on the unlit road can make it very hard to drive on at night. I was holding on to the steering wheel tight and praying to God and the angels for help and safety. Suddenly, I could feel a hand on my shoulder giving me reassurance. I was very surprised and a bit nervous. I badly wanted to look in the rear-view mirror, but I knew that I had to keep my eyes on the road. This gesture from my guardian angel helped immensely, giving me hope that I would arrive home safely. I thanked my angel for the support and for providing me with protection.

My guardian angel and one of the archangels, Michael, helped me out again a few years later. When I was driving my grandson home, I had a weird thought come to my mind. I wondered what I should do if I got into a car accident: Should I call my daughters right away or wait until I knew I was okay? I figured that I should wait to them anything until I knew that I was okay. Before I left my grandson's house, I asked my angels and Michael to be with me on the drive home. I came up to a part in the highway that I did not like. I had turned my head to make sure that no one was turning into my lane from the east. I was travelling about 90 km an hour, heading south.

Suddenly, there was a blur of a vehicle coming from the south and turning right in front of my car so that the driver could go west. At 90 km an hour, I slammed on my brakes the best I could and was told by a spirit or my angels to swing my steering wheel to make the car go into the oncoming lane. This action saved my life. My car landed in the ditch on my side of the road. I blacked out, and when I came to, I was disorientated. I suffered a concussion and a small fracture in my left hand. But I was alive, and I knew that the ANGELS SAVED MY LIFE. I thanked God and the angels for being with me, not only for my sake but also for the young person driving the other car. This person did not have to carry the memory of seriously harming or killing someone on the road due to a lack of attention on her part. My car was hit from the front, but the headlight on my side was intact. The passenger side of the car was all bashed in. The dashboard on that side was pushed in, as well. If I had not listened, my side would have been hit just as badly or worse, and I would have been seriously injured.

Every night before I go to bed, I thank the angels for being with me and protecting me at night. Since I was about 45, I've been thanking them for helping me to get through bad dreams and to lessen the attacks from the lost spirits and entities that occur during the new moon phase.

Acknowledging and getting to know the energies of the Angelic Realm.

As I grew in experiences and learned more about angels, the knowledge that there was another realm and higher state of being became stronger within me. It helped me to understand that we, too, are beautiful beings and that we are loved by God and the angels. I learned that if we push away our guardian angels, they cannot help us, but they can still give us nudges and signs that they are there, ready to help.

There are religions that do not believe in the angelic beings. They may believe in God, but their belief does not go farther than this. It is hard to share with these people some of the beliefs I have now, as they are still at the state of being where the doors are closed to all possibilities, and experiences are limited due to teachings by their religious organization. I have also worked with clients from many different countries and religious/spiritual upbringings and been surprised at how many do believe in the angelic realm. I am tickled pink that I can share my stories with so many people.

Work that angels do:

Angels can show that they are with us by giving us different signs:

-   Angels will appear and share a smell or a message. As I
    was writing this chapter, I started to smell cigarette smoke.
    This reminded me of my friend's mother who passed
    away last summer. Before her passing, I saw that she was
    an earth angel, and that when she crossed over to the
    other side, she would be meeting her angelic team. This
    beautifully woman was on a very tough mission in this

lifetime. Her team was the heavenly angels. To see this in a vision was so beautiful and calming as I knew her transition would be fast. I said thank you to this beautiful earth angel for showing up and letting me know that I was on the right path with this book.

- Angels bring affirmations. People have had dimes appear on the ground right in front of them when they were pondering on a question. These dimes are an affirmation from the angels that things will be okay and that their plans will work out, or that someone that they are worrying about will be okay.

- You may also suddenly see a white feather falling through the air in front of you, either inside or outside. This feather seems to materialize out of nowhere. Another message of support.

- Angels let me know to trust what I am sharing and feeling. When I start to doubt myself while sharing a message during an Intuitive or card reading, I will often get an overwhelming feeling. My body will get tingly and I will be filled with a strong feeling of love and the urge to cry with joy. Tears will come to my eyes and I need to physically readjust to the angelic energy before I can continue with the message. The person that I am working with can see the shift or change that I am experiencing and understand how deeply I am feeling the message. It is very powerful and loving at the same time.

- Angels bring comfort and healing. People have heard the songs of angels in times of despair. The voices of angels and angelic instruments can raise the vibrations of the energy around them. Angelic singing reaches right inside of you and opens the heart and gives back hope and faith.

Please remember:

Angels are helpers of God. They are here to help us and to teach us what unconditional love is all about. When you really need help, please ask your angel to assist you, and do this out loud. Helping people is what they love to do.

Archangel Ariel

Archangel Ariel is connected to the lions and sprites. Ariel means "lion" or "lioness." If Archangel Ariel is around you and trying to get your attention, you may feel or hear the wind or get images of lions.

It is said that Archangel Ariel was connected to King Solomon and works with manifestation, divine magic, and releasing spirits. What do you want to manifest? Remember to ask for your highest good and don't get greedy you will open more doors and have more magical adventures.

When working with Archangel Ariel and the sprites, we work with the waterways: rivers, streams. Helping Mother Earth by healing the water from environmental issues and working with the animal kingdom. Both Archangel Ariel and Archangel Raphael work together with the animals and we can assist by helping provide divine energy to what is required for healing.

Archangel Azrael

Archangel Azrael is known as "Whom God Helps." Archangel Azrael helps people to make the transition from physical life to death. He helps people know that they are safe, and that God is waiting for them on the other side. He will also help family members with the transition and provide the healing energy that they need. He will be there with you when someone dear to you is about to transition over.

Archangel Azrael can also help us out when we are working as grief counsellors. His presence helps us to not absorb the sad energy from those we are counselling and to be in the state of love.

Archangel Chamuel

Archangel Chamuel is a protector of Mother Earth and is one of the seven major archangels. He is here to help us learn how we can change the darker energies back to the light. His presence is strong right now along with Michael's and Raphael's. There is much turmoil in our world and most of it is caused by fighting among those of different nationalities and with different religious beliefs. The control imposed by religion, power and greed is coming to an end. Humans are learning that we need to be able to have our own personal religious or spirituals beliefs and that we must never harm someone else because they don't believe in the same things we do.

Archangel Chamuel is also here to help us in our daily lives; to help us with our life purpose, love life, finding our soul mate, and finding lost items. If you have lost something, just ask for his help. He is here to help us obtain world peace and help us recognize each other as sisters and brothers. If you are wanting to ensure that lower energies are not in your space, please ask for his help.

Archangel Gabriel

Archangel Gabriel's presence is seen by her copper color, and she is known as "God is my Strength." She became known as God's messenger.

Archangel Gabriel is here to help those who want to have children. This can be through pregnancy or by adoption. When this process is easy and worry-free, children will have a better start to life, and many times the birth will be much easier.

Archangel Gabriel is also here to help others spread spiritual messages, whether through music, art, communication, dancing or other means. If a person wants to teach others about spiritual messages, this is the angel to ask for help. She will show you the way and assist with providing opportunities for you. She is there to help us take that step and let go of our fear. This is also the angel to keep in mind when you are working with media, such as radio and television.

Archangel Haniel

Archangel Haniel is known for her light-blue energy. She is known as the "Grace of God' and is here to teach us how we can heal our bodies with the energy of earth's herbal medicines and with the moon's energy. She knows what we need when it comes to natural healing remedies and how they must be prepared. When we practice energy work, we can ask Haniel to bring in the energy of the medicine/herb/crystal that is needed for the client. Or we can ask her what to provide as an option to suggest to the client. (If a practitioner is not properly licensed or trained in herbology or as a Naturopath, they cannot subscribe any kind of medicine.

This angel shows us how to bring grace, beauty, poise and harmony back into our lives. When you need support in a job interview or strength in doing a presentation, this angel will help you. Archangel Haniel can also be asked to help you develop your psychic abilities. These includes clairvoyance, visions, vivid dreams, seeing or hearing something more than once, seeing lights and sparkles, and dreaming of lost ones.

Archangel Jeremiel

Archangel Jeremiel has prophetic visions and helps others develop their visionary abilities. He can also assist with interpreting psychic dreams.

He helps the souls that have crossed over to the other side and assists when going over the records of their past lives. Jeremiel can help you to make changes for the better by helping you to access your past lives and see what has held you back. What changes can you make in this lifetime so that you can clear the energy imprints from unpleasant past experiences? When we take a more positive road, our lives change for the better.

Archangel Jophiel

Archangel Jophiel makes herself known by her pink colours and energies. She is also known as the "Beauty of God".

Archangel Jophiel helps us to see the beauty in the world around us and what can be created. When we change metaphysically and physically, we open ourselves up to greater possibilities and insights. When we are lighter in energy, what happens around us becomes more magical, we think more beautiful and loving thoughts, we are more creative and our ability to manifest gets stronger. Archangel Jophiel teaches us that when we slow down and learn to appreciate what we have and all the beauty in our lives, our health and well-being improve.

Archangel Metatron

Archangel Metatron is known as the "Angel of Presence." Both Archangel Metatron and his brother Sandalphon were mortal men who lived here on planet Earth. He is one of the youngest archangels, as he joined the angels after his time on earth. When you see green and pink lights, that is Archangel Metatron.

He was known as Enoch during his human life but is known to walk with God, as his God energy remained intact when he was on earth. God, seeing this, took Enoch to seventh heaven and gave him his angel wings and status. Archangel Metatron helps keep the Akashic records updated.

Archangel Metatron is here to help us learn more about the Angelic Realm and how we can learn to work with the angels. He loves to help children, especially those who have been labelled as being ADD, autistic and the other sensitive ones. These children have extraordinary gifts and are more connected to the spirit realm than those around them. Metatron would love to see the end of the harsh drugs that these gifted children are being put on. He will help these children learn to use the gifts they have in a healthy and supportive way.

Archangel Michael

Archangel Michael is known to be the "One that is like God." He is here to help dispel the darker energies and toxins that are related to fear. He works with lightworkers to help them with spiritual teachings and healing work. He has helped and inspired many over the years: strong leaders who helped lead people along a better path, and lightworkers such as Brother Jesus when he walked on the earth plane. (I ask for his assistance when doing house and land clearings, and to help escort out those who have walked a path of darkness.)

I ask him to be with me when I am travelling down highways, and we use his sword to help cut cords for spirits that are stuck on this earth plane and hanging around on the roads. He helps us to be stronger and to realize that we do not need to walk in fear, that we are strong when we walk in the heart centre.

He shows us that he is there by his blue and purple lights. Michael is awesome when it comes to helping with electronics, and even things like plumbing. (This, I have personally seen! When I was having a tough time with the sink draining properly, I did a meditation on the flow of the water and asked for his assistance, and within a day or two the pipes were draining a lot better.)

Archangel Raguel

Archangel Raguel is known as the "Friend of God." Archangel Raguel ensures that all the angels in heaven are working together and in harmony, and with the Divine will. He is known to make sure that all are treated fairly, and if one isn't, he will be there to help you increase your personal power and receive the respect you deserve. When you see his pale blue colours, you know he is there to help.

Archangel Raguel is also known as a counsellor; he knows how to help you recharge your batteries and give you the strength you need. This can really come in handy when you are having disagreements with others. He will help to bring the solutions that will benefit both parties.

Archangel Raphael

Archangel Raphael is known as the spiritual healer for humans and animals. He works with healers and teachers to bring forth the energies and teachings for us to learn. His presence will help with stress and in times of anxiety. He will help the natural healer find the right earthly and heavenly remedies for their patient. He can be called upon for guidance during treatments and for getting the education one needs to move forward in this field. He also helps us to open our third eye—the gateway to the spiritual realm.

Archangel Raphael's gentleness with the animal kingdom brings help to animals in need. He will also make sure that suffering animals are brought to the healers who are able to work with them.

Archangel Raphael is known for travelling with you and making sure that travel arrangements go well. If you see an emerald green light or sparkles and flashes, Archangel Raphael might just be around. He also works with Archangel Michael to help spirits cross over to the other side.

Archangel Raziel

Archangel Raziel means "Secret of God." He works closely with God and knows all the secrets about the universe and how everything works together. He is known to have written a book called "The Book of the Angel Raziel," which contains a guide on manifesting and survival. Archangel Raziel gave this book to Adam after he was expelled from the Garden of Eden.

Archangel Raziel can help you when you are developing your psychic skills. He can help you access the higher realms, understand what you are picking up on and help you to see, hear, feel and know. He helps you to connect with the Divine Source and provides guidance. With this, he shows you how you can manifest what you need in life. Archangel Raziel's presence is seen as rainbow stripes and colours.

Archangel Sandalphon

Archangel Sandalphon is Archangel Metatron's twin brother. They both resided on earth before becoming archangels. Archangel Sandalphon is known as the prophet Elijah. His brother was the wise man known as Enoch. There is a story about how when Elijah went to heaven, he went in a chariot pulled by two fiery horses. When he returned to heaven, he became Archangel Sandalphon as a reward for doing so well on earth.

Archangel Sandalphon is here to help deliver our prayers to God. He also helps us to develop our clairaudience. (Clairaudience: to hear messages, whether through sound, music, or noises; to hear someone call your name, or hear a decease relative or angel talking to you.) He loves music and works well with musicians who are stuck or who want to create more music. He will relay his messages through music, and you need to listen carefully to hear him as he is very quiet.

Archangel Uriel

When Archangel Uriel is around, you may see glimpses of pale yellow. He is known as "God's Light." Uriel will come help when you need to see the light in situations where you have become stagnant or blocked. He will bring prophetic messages and sometimes they are warnings. Many of his prophecies have come true. Archangel Uriel teaches us about the power of divine magic.

Archangel Uriel also brings us information on how we can change things through the practice of alchemy, or of changing metal to gold. With this knowledge, we can also manifest into our lives what we require to be of service. Uriel is considered one of the wisest angels. He will be there when you require the right information, or he may be the one that helps to bring you that new idea for your project. He is there when we need help with studying, writing, and further spiritual understanding.

Archangel Uriel can be asked to help with any natural disaster, such as flooding or earthquakes. When you need help to lessen the impact of Mother Nature's harshest weather, call on Uriel and he will be there. He can help to lessen the impact and also help with healing related to the aftermath of severe weather.

Archangel Zadkiel

Archangel Zadkiel is known as the "Righteousness of God." He will protect those who are being used as a pawn for another's use. He stopped Abraham from sacrificing his son.

Archangel Zadkiel and Archangel Michael work together. They help us to see the divinity within us, by showing us that we, too, are of the Divine Source and have the beauty of the love and light in each of us. Archangel Zadkiel helps us to have compassion and unconditional love for ourselves and others. He shows us how we can change negative energy patterns and thoughts that we hold on to. We can transform old energy residue from past situations and move forward with healthier thoughts. If you are having a hard time and not able to let go of old patterns, ask Archangel Zadkiel for his assistance.

Archangel Zadkiel is also here to help us with our memory, whether we are doing a presentation, studying for a test, or just want to improve our memory in general. Just ask his help and you will receive it.

*   *   *

I am so grateful that I got to reconnect with the Angelic Realm as an adult and remembered what my dad had taught me as a child. Angels have been a huge part of my life and have helped me to grow in strength, knowing that I am being looked after. The wisdom they share is a huge blessing. This information is shared with friends, family and clients, and has provided powerful and positive changes in their lives.

If there is someone in my life who is going through a hard time, instead of worrying about them I ask the angels to be with them. This way, I don't bring down my own energy level and add the energy of my worry to their space. The angels will help to lighten their load and provide support. If the person is not open to divine healing energies, then I will just pray for the best outcome for that person.

Ascended Masters

The Ascended Masters work closely with the angels. Many of them have lived on earth and due to their work and achievements were promoted to the status of a master. They now reside in a spirit state and assist mankind during their journeys in this earth. I work with St. Germaine and the violet flame while doing energy work or in workshops. There are a lot of times that I have felt brother Jesus walking beside me and I see him as my brother. I felt it very important share some information on some of these amazing masters. I don't knowingly work with many of them, yet I know that they show up in the treatment room for clients, and with this I am very grateful.

Jesus

Jesus became known healer during his time and is still here to help us. There are many stories about his passing. Some say he died one the cross that he was nailed to. Some say he went into a deep state of meditation when he was nailed to the cross but came back to full state of consciousness and married Mary Madeline and had children with her in France. No matter what the stories were, Jesus became a big part of the teachings in the bible.

Over the years there have been many stories about people seeing Brother Jesus in visions and at certain landmark sites. When this happens, they experienced powerful healing. Jesus's presence can be felt by the feeling of divine energy and love.

Jesus is part of a group called the "Great White Brotherhood". This is a group of ascended masters that work together to bring love and peace back to the world. The members of this group come from countries around the world, India, Africa and Europe. Amazing figures that brought healing to those around them by their kind actions and support to the communities.

Spiritual healers ask for his presence during healing sessions for physical, emotional and spiritual healing. Jesus helps us with communication with God, divine intervention to help us go forward, learn about faith, and helps us to manifest our dreams.

Mary, the Beloved Mother

Also know as Mother Mary, Virgin Mary, Queen of the Angels. Mother Mary became a part of many stories and theories. Compiled stories said that she is the mother of Jesus and the stepmother for Josephs other 5 children. Mother Mary had a tough life working hard to help the family and her husband Joseph who was a wood worker. She is was very patient with an angelic presence.

Her presence today is very powerful as she is working with the light workers and healers on earth to provide a better life for the Indigo and Crystal children. She knows that these children don't do well with the chemicals in the foods and in the environment. The vibration of these children is very high and can't handle the toxins, vaccinations and altered food.

For those that call out loud for help, their prayers will be heard. This beautiful angel and sister can teach us about compassion for ourselves and others around us. She shares how the compassion can fill our hearts full of the divine essence of pure love. She helps with healings, answers prayers, and the children of this planet.

Mary Magdalene

Mary Magdalene represents the Divine Feminine energy. She helps with fidelity with family, friends and our partners. She was married to Jesus in on of her lifetimes. The story is that hey lived in France and had children together.

Mary is here to help with our environment, equality and to help us heal from abuse. Her energy and lessons can provide us with inner confidence and strength, compassion and openness.

St Germaine (Comte de Saint-Germaine)

I am excited to share this information about St. Germaine. He came to me several years ago while I was doing a Reiki attunement, and he showed me how the violet flame needed to be incorporated into the attunement for the students. A few months later I found out who St. Germaine was. and this validated what I was shown to do during the attunements. Now I invite him in during Reiki classes that I teach for support for all of us.

St. Germaine was an actual human, like brother Jesus, that walk this earth. He was known to live in France and born around 1690 and 1710. St. Germaine was known among the wealthy for the work he did. He was an artist, played the violin, spoke several languages, and deeply involved with the spiritual teachings and healing. He did psychic readings, studied and taught about alchemy.

St. Germain and Archangel Michael work closely together, sharing their amazing protection and guidance. Things that St. Germain helps with are: alchemy, courage, showing us what direction to go in and life purpose. He shows us how we are protected and how to keep our spaces clearing. We can also use alchemy to manifest the dreams of our hearts.

St. John of God

St. John of God is known for his work with the mental and physically ill people. He is there to support them and help them out. He also works with those that have problems with their hearts.

After moving to Spain, he worked as a shepherd, then a soldier and later sold books while traveling. After he heard a speech, he gave away his belongings and was either sent to or submitted himself to the psychiatric ward of a hospital. Here he learnt how bad it was for those that were trying to get better and realized how bad the conditions were. From there he went to live on the streets and the hardships there showed him compassion for those who are homeless and with no proper assistance to get well. He started a safe place called `The Hospitaller Order of Saint John of God``. This was a place for those who were mentally and physically ill and did not have the funds for health care. He later bought a place in Granada Spain to offer the same service.

When people came in for help, he was there to help bath them, feed them and sat and prayed with them. St. John of God was an empath that understood what other people were feeling and going through. At this shelter, he earned his name that of a Saint. St. John of God can help us with the following: mentally and physical challenges, healing, when we are in the hospital, and assistance in our spiritual pursuits.

CHAPTER 6

Fairy Realm

I'm sitting here at the end of September 2018, dreaming of the Fairy Realm and remembering all the times the fairies have presented themselves to me. From seeing distinctive faces within the mind's eye while learning about the Akashic records, to feeling their presence with either a sneeze or a cold sensation in my lower body, I have had many such experiences. Fairies have been with us, I believe, since the beginning of life on Mother Earth. The fairies/fae are known as being the earth's angels and guardians. They are a high vibrational being of the light and are connected to the energies of the earth. They can be found in the fourth to fifth dimensions.

Brownies, elves, fairies, gnomes, goblins, leprechauns, mermaids, nymphs, pixies, sprites and unicorns are all part of the Fairy Realm. They work with Mother Earth, the waterways and plants. They are experts when it comes to plant medicine and will help healers during their sessions with clients.

After I had moved into an amazing house in Cochrane with a huge yard, I was told that I had a lot of fairies in the gardens. It was not until I had been practising Reiki for a while, that I was able to tell that they were around. When the fairies were connected strongly with a client, the bottoms of my legs would get quite cold. Sometimes while teaching the Reiki course, the fairies would join in on the energy. There were many times that fairies would come in with their human friends for the Reiki workshop. During the Reiki attunement for these students, I would need to ask the fairies to go play for a bit, as this was my time to focus on the students and they could come help us later during the class.

When I became aware that there truly were fairies existing here, too, I started to feel their energy as I went for walks. During my walks, especially walks in the forest or in heavily treed parks, I would pick up on the shift in the energy. Sometimes it felt like I was about to walk through a doorway or an invisible arbour, from one energy field into another. Each time this energy was presented, I would stop and recalibrate my energy field to what I was picking up on. Then I would move forward into the Fairy Realm.

There is a provincial park close to town that has very strong fairy energy. So many times, I have felt the shift and known that I had entered another realm. The energy could be seen in pictures that I took, and the trees would look blurry. Along one hill, I was not allowed to take a picture; the camera on my phone would not work properly. The camera would not click, and no matter what I tried to do the picture could not be taken. Something was energetically taking place there and it was not meant to be seen by the human eye. I took that as a sign that sometimes the other realms needed their privacy, and this was to be respected, especially if we wanted to be welcomed back. Also, in this area, I was guided to stay on the path and not allow my arm or my body to go into the energy that I was sensing there. It felt like a huge bubble to the right side of me. Not many people I know have felt that same shift in the energy that I have, yet they know that the fairies are present. My partner is getting used to me stopping along paths to ask for permission to enter properly.

The Fairy That Hid in the Amethyst

I used to believe that fairies could do no wrong and that they were the same as the angels. I now know that fairies could also be like humans, in that they can become lost and cause undue distress to others or the environment. This, I found out one day when I went to visit a friend who worked in the crystal store where I was working at that time. She shared that a young boy and his mom had been in the store. The boy felt that there was something or someone stuck in a piece of amethyst. My friend tried washing the amethyst to clear it, but this did not seem to be working.

When I held the amethyst, I knew that a fairy was stuck within the amethyst. With some energy work, I was able to free the fairy and was very surprised to see Archangel Michael suddenly there standing beside the fairy. The fairy grabbed her wand and went off with Michael. I realized then that this little fairy had gotten herself into some trouble and was hiding in the stone, hoping she wouldn't be found. Humans, like fairies, have free will; they can also make good or not-so-good choices. When the little one does the work to rectify what she has done, I believe she will be back and will be a lot more careful next time.

The Fairy Delegate

In the summer of 2017, I met two amazing souls at the Calgary Folk Festival. They came to my booth for some energy work. WOW! The sessions with these two opened my eyes even more; they gave me a stronger understanding of how we really are working in different realms. For some of us, we do this unknowingly.

The young man I met works in the Fairy Realm (he was doing this work unknowingly), as a delegate among the different groups: fairies, elves, gnomes, etc. His job is to keep the peace and to ensure that rules and regulations are being upheld. If there is disharmony in a sector, he is called in to settle matters and bring resolution and peace back to the area. This is done in the fairy dimension, and I believe, in his dream time, unknowingly. The next day, when he came back for more energy work, he was amazed at what he felt and saw and wanted to learn more.

How does one do this without knowing? We are energetic beings: the essence of our soul is immense and expansive. We are here in our waking hours and there in dream time. We visit our homeland in both states and work in unison with other beings and dimensions, yet we still reside in the human vessel. We can be in several places at once, knowingly and unknowingly. I have been told this several times: that I travel many places and show up in people's dreams when they need help or protection. We are all very connected.

The Fairy Seamstress

Back to the folk festival . . .

The young woman who the fellow was with also showed me something very magical. When I was working with her during an energy session, I saw her sewing magic and protection tools into the clothing and accessories of the Fairy Realm, and she was doing this for the dragons, too. She did this in the dream state, and I wondered if she was a fairy in another lifetime. This young gal helped me to make a stronger connection with the Fairy Realm, and the memories and the energies I experienced were so beautiful that I had joyous tears running down my face.

As I shared what I saw during the session with her, I could see, in my mind's eye, a baby dragon on her left shoulder. Suddenly, I realized that the little dragon was hiding two other babies. They were holding on to each other's tails and hanging down the young woman's back. After a bit, they all sat on her shoulder together. This young woman was living in two dimensions, unknowingly. In real life, she is a seamstress who sews beautiful, magical, fairy-like clothing to sell at markets.

Fairy Magic for the Oldest Child

When I do a clearing in a house, I have no information about the family and very little information on events that have happened before I get the call to do the clearing. During some of the house clearings that I do, fairies show up and make themselves present. They let me know which of the children in the house they play with, who they are protecting, and they also let me know if boundaries need to be set in the home regarding the different dimensions or spirit realm. When I ask if a certain child is sensitive or connected to the fairies, the parents will be honest and let me know if I am right, or if it is another child who is.

In this home where three children resided, the fairies worked mostly with the oldest child. This child had a hard time with confidence as someone in her life shattered her faith and sense of well-being. Working with the Fairy Realm can help a person get stronger and allow one's imagination to grow. This is something humans have been gradually losing with all the advances in technology and strict "Don't talk about that; people will think you're crazy" attitudes. Thankfully, the girl's mother was very aware of the fairy connection and fully supported it. When I shared with the young woman how strong her connection to the Fairy Realm really was and how she could work with the fairies, her eyes lit up. I mentioned some of the ways that the fairies could help to give her strength each day.

The Fairy Creek

When I was doing a house and land clearing north of Cochrane, Alberta, I could sense the presence of the Fairy Realm. The energy was very strong and drew my attention to a little creek that runs through the property. The youngest child who lived there would build fairy gardens with her mom in the springtime. This little girl would spend hours outside (they live in the country), building bridges and homes for the fairies. What a magical way to spend a day when you are on your own. She could see and hear the fairies speaking and knew what they needed for their village, and they, in turn, warned her of any upcoming danger. The amethyst from which I had freed the lost fairy came out to this land to be looked after. I knew it belonged there and not in my home. The young girl put the amethyst on her windowsill, which faces the creek.

Rainbow Magic for the Fairies and the Land

I was reminded of a drive that I went on in 2016 with my brother, in Australia, to a town that I was told by a spirit not to go to. I could feel in my gut that going there would not be a good idea, as we would be treading on territory that carried heavy energy. However, I finally agreed and went for the drive. As we got closer to the town, we were slowed down by a road construction crew. I looked ahead and saw a lot of garbage along the road and wondered where the pride of this community was. What were we driving into?

I made my brother promise that if I told him to stop and leave town, that he needed to do so, and that I did not want any arguments about this. I told him that if he did not agree, I would get out of the car right then and there. Driving into town, I could feel a strange energy, different from what I felt before. It felt unsettling.

As we drove through a residential neighbourhood where youth were playing, we received a very unwelcome response from one of them. This town consisted of both white immigrants and Aboriginal folk. We went another block or so and I told my brother it was time to go.

As we were leaving town, I went into energy mode and asked for assistance from God, the elders of the land, the angels and the Fairy Realm to help heal the land and the inhabitants. I knew that we could only do so much and the rest was up to the landowners. As I had my eyes closed, I asked that the land be blessed with all the healing colours of the rainbow. I saw a fairy go up to a rainbow of energy in order to re-ignite her wand. She then flew off, blessing the land, plants and flowers with the rainbow colours. What an amazing vision to have.

Later, after I got back to where I was staying, I told someone where we had gone. They were shocked to hear that I was taken there, as the landowners and immigrants were not at peace. There was also a lot of bad and good medicine there. It was a constant battle between the two. As I travelled down the coastline, I thought of that town often and prayed for peace and love to come to the community and to heal, on a soul level, everyone involved. Again, I thanked the fairies for their part in the healing work. The fairy with her rainbow wand was grateful to see the flora shine again.

Work that the fairies do:

- Fairies help to maintain Mother Earth; they are the earth's keepers.
- They ensure that proper conditions are met for the flora in the areas in which they dwell. The fairies are the permaculture team of the earth. When something has been done to harm their home, they work overtime to ensure that the balance is maintained again.
- Fairies will work with humans when they are asked, and upon approval, one can be accepted into their realm. They will work with us to do land clearings and help to change

the energy of negative imprints that have been left behind. Since humans are the cause of many of the imprints, the human must initiate the change and ask for help.

- The fairies also work with the animals. They help the ones that have been hurt and bring in the energy medicines for them.

Elves

My First Elf Visit

Another encounter with the Fairy Realm occurred in 2016. During a session with a client, my whole right side got quite cold. I shared that the Fairy Realm was with her, and the energy was very strong. I told this client that the fairy energy was there working with her, not knowing that the elves were there for her protection.

Second Elf Visit - For My Protection

About two days later, I went for a drive with a friend through the hills west of the town I live in. I believe that we were quite close to the mountains. The friend was driving recklessly, going a bit too fast down the road, and there were still patches of snow and ice.

I was getting quite scared and the driver was ignoring my pleas to slow down. I closed my eyes and asked the fairies to please help me out. I went into healing energy mode and prayed silently for our safety, as I did not want to crash on the hillside or slide down the cliff. Suddenly, my right side became icy cold. My truck window was closed, and I knew that someone was there for me. A moment later, the truck jolted as if it ran over something, and the driver slowed right down. The rest of the drive was quiet and more relaxing.

The next day, when the driver went to his truck, one of his tires was flat. Later in the day, he went to pick up the truck from the mechanic and was shown what had been stuck in the tire. It was an arrow-shaped rock. I truly believe an elf shot an arrow at the tire to slow down the truck for me. About one year later, I learned that elves are quite tall, and they are protectors. This was why my whole right side went cold in the truck and I knew that I was being energetically safeguarded. I received so many blessings that day, and I thank both the fairies and the elves for their protection.

Work that the elves do:

- The elves are the protectors of the Fairy Realm. They prefer to live in peace and with the land, but when there is chaos, they will be the first ones at your side to help.

- The elves are also protectors of the animals and humans that are lovingly connected to their realm. A human must be invited in, and that human must show respect for the land and the flora.

Sprites

In a home where I was doing another clearing, I was shown that the child living there was being bothered by a sprite. The sprite would cause havoc and make life hard for the little boy. I told the parent that the child needed to set boundaries. While I was there, I let the sprite know that he needed to behave, or he would be escorted out ASAP. I know that sprite heard me. Sprites are known for causing mischief.

*   *   *

The Fairy Realm shows up in my life almost daily. When they are giving me an affirmation for something that I am thinking of, I have the urge to sneeze, and most times I do. The sneeze is from the beautiful earth energy and soil that tickles one's nose.

Fairies love to play with my friends' cat by bugging him and making him twitch. It is really fun to watch. The cat tries to look annoyed, but I know he loves it. My baby dragon friends will often join the fairies, which makes for even more mischief. One morning, the cat would not sit on the windowsill and was mewing at whatever was there. I believe both the fairies and dragons were up there. As soon as we asked that they move so that the cat could have his perch back, the cat jumped up on the windowsill.

Fairies love to play, work, heal and look after their plant folk. They know the medicines of the land and know what all the plants need to survive. They have no patience for those who litter or leave carnage behind. There is a form of Universal Law that looks after those who have no respect for Mother Earth.

There are many times when I see fairy wings on humans; in my minds eye I can see the colours and how big they are. When I get to see these fairy folk, tears of joy come to my eyes and I lovingly share what I see. This usually brings joy to the receiver and brings a beautiful light to their eyes. Their eyes will start to twinkle. The person usually shares with me how they love the fairies and their gardens. We are very grateful for these amazing spiritual beings that have joined us in human form.

Chapter 7

Entering the Dragon World

As we travel from our root chakra to our crown chakra, we are learning how to be connected to Mother Earth and survive in the human bodies that we were given to live in.

We also learn how to reconnect with the heavens and other galaxies, as our true memories come back into existence.

Getting Introduced to My Dragon

February 2010

In 2009, the movie *Avatar* came out and I saw it in February 2010 for my fiftieth birthday. If felt like I was there, flying through the forest, remembering what the earth was like in the beginning. Lush foliage, magical plants with fluorescent colours that we see in the fish at the bottom of the ocean. The Avatars were flying on dragons and it felt so real watching the movie. I told my daughter that I wanted to be an Avatar when I finished growing up. My daughter told me to calm down; this was just a movie. The movie had me feeling like it was a lot more than that, and that life in another time was so different from what it is now. Later in the same year, I had confirmations for what I was picking up on energetically.

May 2010

I was invited to go to a dragon meditation with a good friend. This was a meditation to help us to meet our dragons. It sounded like fun and I was curious and wondered how many other people really believed in dragons. During the meditation I did not see much. At the end of the evening, I knew there was a dragon with me, but I could not see him. I didn't know how big he was or what colour he was; I just knew he was there. I was sad, as everyone else was able to see their dragons. But I still believed and kept wondering what it would take for me to meet my dragon.

November 2010

Before I went to Australia in 2010, my body was shifting energetically and there were times when I could feel the adrenaline going wild in my legs. I felt nervous and scared, yet extremely excited, as I was going to go visit my dad's homeland. A dear friend said that my body was getting ready for the changes that were coming. As I was boarding the plane, I asked my dragon friend to fly with me as I was petrified of the long flight ahead, being away from my daughters for the first time and being over the ocean for so many hours. I visualized a dragon flying alongside the plane and sitting on top of it. I knew that the energy of this amazing fellow was keeping us all safe and providing me with a sense of calm.

December 2010

When I finally arrived at my brother's home to stay for two weeks, the energy was getting stronger around me and my legs were feeling a lot of neat things. When I met one of his friends, I knew right away that this friend had a red dragon with him. I had not even met mine yet. This knowing was magical and after seeing that fellow's dragon in my mind's eye, my excitement was building. I was told by my spirit guide to share this information about the dragon and the fellow appreciated it. This was the first time that I saw a dragon with someone.

January 2017

I was asked to do a house clearing for a family member in the city. There was something in the kitchen that was scaring the youngest child. I did the energy work that was needed to clear out the heavy energy. This time, I did not see what it was, but I knew that it felt mean and untrustworthy. The home was in a very rough neighbourhood where the sounds of gunshots were heard almost daily. A month or so later, I saw a little green-and-orange dragon on the youngest child's shoulder. while Later, when I saw him again, he asked me if the dragon was still there. I said "Yes!" Unfortunately, sometimes family dynamics don't let the little ones grow up with magic in their hearts and they are told to forget what they see and experience. I know this little one will see again when he gets older.

July 2017

In the summer of 2017, I finally saw my dragon friend. I was at a Viking history event that was taking place outside the library in the town where I lived, a few blocks away from my house. I watched the sword fighting for a tiny bit, but I don't like violence so wandered off to see the merchandise booths. I came to a booth that was selling silver pendants and some leatherwork. I saw a pendant with a dragon and other objects with Celtic symbols.

I took a good look at the fellow at the booth and I knew him. My soul knew him from another lifetime, not this one. Suddenly, I felt and saw within my mind's eye this HUGE red dragon on my right side. This dragon was mad and walked a few feet in front of me so he could be seen by something that was beside the fellow at the booth. This was my dragon! It had long, red, old-man tentacles (beard strands that show the age of a dragon). I was shocked, awed and surprised. The energy of my friend dragon was so strong that it took me a few days to remember what happened at the booth, and for the memory of what I saw to anchor in my mind. I met my dragon again!

When I could finally remember clearly what happened, I shared the information with a fellow healer who attended the same market. She saw him in a vision and said he was ancient—old as dirt—red, and battle-scarred. She found a picture that resembled him. Wow. Later, when I was doing energy work for this friend, she remembered working with the dragons at another time. There were tears in her eyes. Some of the memories were overwhelmingly sad, as something unpleasant happened to the dragons when she was with them in that lifetime.

February 2018

A dream I'd had for several years was to attend the Brisbane MindBodySpirit Festival, and I was blessed to be able to do so at the end of February 2018. Taking my first two books overseas to Australia and being able to do energy work and readings during the expo went from being a dream to a reality. A dear friend of mine helped me to get to the expo and was able to share a booth with me. He had some of his amazing artwork on the walls. He had started painting the year before on a multidimensional level. The energy from these pictures was strong and helped bring up the vibration in the booth and the building. There were a lot of people who were drawn to the energy that we were working in. During quiet moments at the expo, we talked about dragons and fairy energy.

When I was planning this amazing trip, my plans did not go further than the first week there. After the expo, when I realized I had maybe not planned properly, I got quite discouraged and wondered if I had made the right choice to stay in Australia for a month. Was this too long? What was I doing? Was I kidding myself and doing something that was not for my highest good? Little did I know that I was following divine guidance and doing exactly what was planned by the universe.

After looking at my plane ticket information, I realized that I needed to stay longer. Then I reminded myself that this trip there was also a reason for celebration. At the end of October in 2017, I had my second book published. This book is an amazing encyclopedia of healing with energy work, and talks about Mother Nature's medicines, using food, herbs and essential oils, among other things. The book is called *Essentials for Natural Healing*.

For a week I got to stay in Toowoomba, west of Brisbane, at my cousin's place. The weather there was a bit cooler, but it was so relaxing. The time I spent there, I was able to fully relax and unwind from the last year or so of huge changes in my life. It was also there that I got to learn more about the Dragonfae and the lessons of the phoenix.

While working with my new set of Dragonfae oracle cards that I found in Toowoomba, I started to think about all the dimensions that I had been able to work with over the years. In 2017, a new friend and fellow healer shared that I was working on a multidimensional level; I was accessing six of the 12 dimensions. When I first stepped into the healing room that I created several years ago, I stated out loud that only those of the love and light were able to be in the healing room to assist. I knew little about what I was asking, yet at the same time I was setting boundaries and I wanted to be safe.

As I worked with the Dragonfae cards, I was thinking about how many realms and groups I had worked with and those that had assisted during energy sessions for my clients, family and friends. These cards had many lessons for me; little did I know what would show up about a week later.

After my stay in Toowoomba, I headed back to Petrie, taking the Greyhound bus to Brisbane and then the train the rest of the way. As I journeyed back, I observed the changes in the landscape and daydreamed about life in general and saw all the blessings of what was, what is and what will be. Still unsure about the rest of my journey there. I did know that my friend and his girlfriend were interested in taking the level one Usui Reiki course and it was a blessing to know that he wanted me to teach them. He had also mentioned my attending the Westside Market in Brisbane with him. There was a person I had met at the expo who was interested in a reading and this person lived close to the market, so I was looking forward to seeing her again.

My dear friend invited me back to stay at his place in Petrie, just north of Brisbane. I love this part of the country: the rolling green hills, winding roads, valleys, giant trees, vines, and the many different flowers and tropical birds. Each day that I got up, my heart was filled with love and blessings as I heard the birds and smelled the sweet aroma in the air. The air there is different from here in Alberta, Canada. It is sweet from the fragrance of the flowers. I went for a lot of walks, drew pictures and painted tags for my batik bags that I create. I relaxed and enjoyed the blessings that were waiting for me. I also got to attend some of the markets there, in Brisbane and Eumundi (which is north of Brisbane).

In the yard, my friend had a healing circle that had created the energy of a portal. There was a circle of crystals with rose quartz and clear quartz. The energy from this portal was strong, and I spent a lot of time sitting beside it. There was hearsay that this portal could be on a dragon ley line that came up from Brisbane. I wondered if this was the same path of the dream serpent in Byron Bay, south of Brisbane? A couple of times, as I sat in the portal, I was looking forward to my next visit there. What would I see and experience then?

This brings me to the next few days and the events that unfolded that led to my writing my third book and sharing what multidimensional healing is. I wrote the following in my journal:

March 11, 2018

When I was walking down the stairs to the main level at my friend's house to make a coffee in the morning, I got a strong feeling that I was to write a third book and I knew that it was to be anchored in while in Australia. As soon as I saw this, I got a huge truth shiver. I was not quite sure what this book was to be about, but knew my trip here got the book anchored in for me. At this time, I also realized that Australia was my place of huge energetic activations.

March 12, 2018

Today, I attended a reading by a friend and artist, a medicine man from Papua, New Guinea. During the reading, he shared that I was to write the third book, an affirmation of what I saw yesterday. The medicine man also shared that he worked energetically with his clients before and after the readings and let me know that I was going through another huge transformation and will be able to let go of a habit that I picked up as a teen. His messages came from a spirit and he also used the Australian animal cards that he created.

Later that day, when I sat down with my Dragonfae oracle cards, again I had a strong feeling that this book was to be about healing with the different dimensions. Right then, I realized that I needed to learn more about what I have been working with during treatments for my clients. After sending some texts to a good friend in Didsbury, Alberta, I started to get more affirmations on this. My friend said she was excited to see the results and excited for my next adventure.

The following night, I dreamed about the spider. My dreams about animals while in Australia on this trip have been another realization about the ways we can access information and receive the messages that we need to move forward. The message I got from the spider was: "To write creatively without limits. Be inspired by nature." This message reminded me of the pictures that I have been drawing of the animals and plants. This led me to going through my journal and highlighting experiences that I have had over the years which occurred during healing sessions and in daily life. All of this is known as Natural Healing.

March 13, 2018

My friend was drawn to take me to Ngungun, one of the Glass House Mountains in Australia, north of Petrie, Queensland. We started to walk up a path that went through a lot of trees and some of the trees had thick trunks and were extremely tall. As we were walking up the path, I started yawning—huge yawns, energy-release yawns. I asked the spirits if this energy work was being down for the earth. I heard a "no." I asked if it was for someone else who was there on the path. I heard another "no." Then I asked if this healing was for me, and I heard a "yes." That was when I knew I was brought to this place by spirit, and that my friend was listening to his guidance as he knew a lot more about the land and history than I did.

As we continued to walk up the path, I saw to the right of me a huge rock formation. At the top of this formation was a cave to the northern side of it. Toward the bottom, there were some ledges that one could sit on or walk along. I said to my friend that I had a strong feeling that a tribe/clan lived there at one time. He asked how I would know this. I shared that it was a very strong feeling that I was getting and that the cave would have been a good shelter, as it was above ground level and had less chance of being flooded in the rains.

At the top of the mountain, my breath was taken away. I could see in all directions the lush green bush, the small mountains, and the farms that were growing tropical crops for food. In one direction, my friend pointed and shared that a mountain to the east of us was a meeting place for the elders. As he said this, I knew that the mountain was also a lookout point for the dragons. This beautiful country was lush with water, rich soil and heat, and when the winds blew, change was coming in. Earth, wind, fire and air: the necessities of abundant food and good health. The memories were coming back: dragons, medicines of the earth, soul family.

We did not stay long at the top. My friend was drawn to go back to the cave we saw. He, too, had a strong sense of dragon energy around the cave and was anxious to return to it. This dragon energy was something we both felt when we went past the cave on the way up the hill but did not share with each other until we were heading back. When we got there, he walked up to the cave's entrance and laid on the ground. I stayed at the bottom, as I was worried about what could be living in the cave, and if there was something living there, would it be friendly? I know that there are a lot of snakes and spiders in this beautiful country.

I found a ledge to sit on and got comfortable, but right away I knew that I had to take my sandals off. When I dug my toes into the earth and started to feel the energy of Mother Earth and the cave foundation, I was briefly taken back to the time that we existed and lived in this part of the land. Tears were pouring down my face as I experienced love for the earth and the medicines that grew from the soil with the assistance of the warmth of the sun. To get my feet dirty in the soil was the most pleasurable sensation, and I remember feeling grounded and connected with the seasons.

In a vision, I saw my friend: he was a watcher of the weather and knew what energies were coming into our territory. He was leading a group of people to teach them about the elements, and how to detect the changes in the weather. I believe he was also a tracker for the hunters who would bring food back to the clan. In the groups that went hunting, there was also a collector of herbs and the berries that grew farther from the camp/cave. I saw myself gathering herbs, cooking meals with them and making tinctures for those that were sick, or to store for use when we needed them.

The earth, the plants, the stones, the water, the sun and the wind were—and still are—the best medicine, not only for the body, but also for the soul. Placing my hands into the waters brought forth information. Holding on to the stones brought the medicines of the earth and the universe. Some stones were used to transport knowledge, both energetically and by downloading information into the right receivers. Knowledge shared from other dimensions is sacred. No matter what the information is, no matter what rock or plant I work with, the energy and healing properties were gratefully received and cherished. This was a magical way to spend part of my last week in Australia.

Later, I found out that this cave is now called Dayman's Cave. The entrance to the cave in a picture that I found, appears to be in the shape of a heart.

June 2018

While at a gathering that I was invited to, I showed a dear friend a picture that I had taken at a campsite. In this picture was a blue ray emanating from the earth like a pillar. I was then told about Blue, who is a protector like Archangel Michael, yet he works with the waterways and the energies/ spirits/entities that are connected to the earth plane.

This friend is also a fellow healer who helped me to get better connected with the dimensions and the beginning of time on this planet called Mother Earth. She can access the dimensions and help people to get connected to their original homes and the realms/ dimensions that they are working with knowingly or unknowingly.

When she tuned into my energy field, she saw me at the beginning of the time of human existence on this planet. She saw me in a cave and working with the earth medicines. I know my original star planet is a long away from here, yet Mother Earth now feels like home. When she saw me, I was living at a time when earth was like a tropical paradise. Beautiful plants and lush foliage, huge trees, dragons, and mystical creatures all coexisted with us and we had homes where we felt safe and ample food that nourished us. We knew which medicines and foods would sustain us. Again, my dragon friend was with me and helped me travel between the dimensions.

My friend shared that when I was driving on the road, I needed to ask Red (my dragon) to keep the energy clear around me as we travelled together. Blue and Archangel Michael also travels with us and we all help heal the imprints in the land, energetically shift the imprints and help spirits cross over to the other side. I also ask all three of them to be with me when I do house clearings.

August 2018

Meeting my friend's dragon was another humbling event and powerful experience. His dragon appeared in front of me in my mind's eye. The dragon came right up to me in a vision so that I could see him. His head is white, the white part continuing to the chest. The rest of the body is a cobalt blue. A couple of months later, I saw that there was a silver colour on the outside of the scales on the body. Just seeing the colouring right now as I am typing, there is cobalt blue outlining the scales on its head. The dragon has shown himself about three times, on different days, to make sure that I did not forget who he was and that he was very present in my partner's life. It was fun to share what I saw. Now when we go for drives in the country, his dragon sits on top of the car and mine flies along my side of the car.

During a meditation, I asked to be shown where my dragon and I started on this planet. There were five of us, each with a dragon. Mine being red, it turns out that I am from the southern hemisphere in Central Australia. In another life, I lived along the eastern coast in the Ngungun area. There were four other dragons in the region. The was an alliance among them and they all worked together to share news and provide protection. This service they provided is the same as clans sending smoke signals or runners to relay news to the next clan.

The white dragon was on the southern coast, close to the mountains where the weather is cooler. There was a blue dragon on the northern coast. The dark green dragon was on the eastern coast where the foliage and fairy energy is strong, and the orange dragon was on the western coast of Australia.

When I look into the past, I know that we were seeded here to start a new civilization and that we needed protection and access to information from our homes. Our position as dragon keepers was not easy, and we had a lot of responsibility. It was a great honour. We were also connected to the Fairy Realm, which could be seen a lot easier at that time.

Again, the dragons were our messengers and shared news and transported goods when necessary. They were able to cloak themselves and go back home to our origins or home planets through portals that were created for speedy and safe travel. This also enabled medicines to be brought back in a hurry when needed. Dragons were able to mingle with each other and eggs were laid containing babies that later joined us, but this was about 100 years in the future to ensure that the dragon energy was anchored in and the dragons were adapted to the climate here on Mother Earth. The eggs of the dragons were well protected, as there were predators and the eggs were not to get into the wrong hands. Life for all beings was sacred.

When the humans were seeded on earth, the dragon energy was established, and the humans that they were to work with were selected by the Divine Source. Images of these great flying beasts would come in dream time, then later in visions for the soon-to-be dragon keepers. Both the dragon and their human took their time getting acquainted so that each respected the other's presence, knowledge and space. The energy of each dragon and human was different and they both needed to be attuned to each other in order to successfully travel together in dream time to the other dimensions and in space. Did humans bring their dragons? Did they know ahead of time that their dragons were going to be here? The humans of the time were medicine people and worked with the realms and Mother Earth's plants and medicines. The chosen ones knew that they needed to be humble and work with no ego and for the betterment of the planet and their community.

Dragon lore was created by those who saw and felt the energies, and sometimes by those who worked with the dragons. Stories were shared and passed down, some true and some not true. Those who consumed too many spirits (intoxicating substances), even in the early times, created delusional stories about dragons to compensate for their own poor actions at the time of intoxication.

April 2019

As I was lying in bed the night before, I felt an energy by my side. I looked to see if it was the cat, and it wasn't. I asked the spirits who was there, and I got a strong image of a baby dragon. The image was very sharp and detailed, something a person could not forget. I knew that I now had a baby dragon with me.

I had been procrastinating about going into the city to drop off some books and knew that today was the day. I was drawn to go into a store that stocked both of my books and the owner was in that day. We started to chat, and I finally asked her, "Do you believe in dragons?" The answer I got not only blew me away, but also affirmed why I was drawn to go into the city that day. This amazing practitioner told me what happened to her in the morning before coming to work.

She was drawn to go into the Akashic records, something that she rarely does, and a practice that I do for my clients. When she went energetically into the records, she was handed a book and it was opened to a specific chapter. There was a flame that came out, then a wee dragon. The baby dragon was being held back by a chain that she knew she needed to release. She looked at me and said she wondered why she needed to do this work in the morning and just realized it was for me. She told me that I had been a dragon keeper in another lifetime, and that I should now have two baby dragons with me, along with Red. The whole time while I was talking and listening, I could feel a tugging at my purse, yet nothing visible was there. Right away, I knew that this was the baby dragon I saw last night in a vision. I have felt the same tug at my purse a few times since then, so I know it is the little dragons.

More Information on Dragons

When doing research, I tried to find out which dimension dragons come from. One site said the sixth dimension and another the tenth. I truly believe that dragons have existed both in solid physical form and in energy form. I truly believe in the dragon energy and know that they were here in the physical form on the earth plane at one time in history. A dear friend shared that dragons in their physical form disappeared when Atlantis went down.

Some channelled information about dragons:

Dragons are as pure of heart as the human can be, though some become lost souls as humans do. They are great protectors and able to take us to other places in the universe, between the realms and around Mother Earth.

They love to fly around the hills and mountains. This provides an amazing raceway and provides the opportunity to practise flying skills. When a person travels over the land and among the hills, one can see in the mind's eye, the path that they fly, and sense the excitement as the dragons fly around the hills playing hide and seek. I giggle each time these images come into my mind.

Dragons are trained to use their fire properly. A dragon's breath/ fire can be as damaging as human words when they are used to hurt someone. They are taught when to use their fire and when it is unhealthy and unsafe for all those concerned. Their breath can help to heat food and water when a glowing fire is not safe due to arid conditions or if one needs to stay hidden.

The underneath of a dragon's scales is quite light and transparent when the dragon is young. As the dragon gets older, this skin gets darker and thicker.

Dragon size and appearance:

When they are very young, baby dragons can be seen sitting on the shoulders of their human. They can be quite mischievous and love to have fun and tease. The first time I saw this, I saw one on the shoulder of a friend and then caught the other two hanging off the tail of the first one and hiding behind my friend. The little ones were cheeky and fun to watch. This vision had me giggling like a little girl.

The young dragon (what would be a teenager in human years) stands from knee-high to waist-high next to an adult human.

The adults and ancient dragons are huge. Depending on the type of dragon, they can be twenty times the size of humans and bigger.

You can often find the babies with old souls, as they tend to be the trainers or elders who provide a safe place for them. Yet, I have seen dragons teamed with a human soul that is similar to the age of the dragon's soul. For example: one of my soul brothers has a huge red dragon. Some of the scales of the dragon have gold on them. I'm not certain what that means, but I'm sure I will be shown in due time. I know my soul brother's soul is as old as his dragon. His girlfriend's dragon is much younger, as she is still a young soul and just learning.

I know my grandchildren are old souls, yet the youngest one has a little dragon with him. What comes to mind is that little dragons love the energy of children, as children still love to play and are innocent and so loving. I'm looking forward to the day that my grandchild sees the other dimensions again. He also knows how to work with portals. He has a lot to teach me when the time comes.

When dragons are in flight in the universe or going through the various dimensions, they wear a white cloak. This cloak makes the dragon and his/her rider appear as a falling star or comet. When I saw my friend's dragon beside him, the dragon was red. Yet when his dragon was circling the portal of light, he was white.

Humbleness is necessary for all of us, including dragons. One does not worship dragons, and one's dragon will not worship its human. Both need to be pure of heart, honour and respect each other's presence and not become dependent on each other. Both human and dragon need to have space and one's own power. We are here to work together as a team.

Learning to Work and Heal with Dragons

In April 2018, I went to the healing room and pulled a Dragonfae card. This one was "Chenguang": *be light of heart.* He is a Dragonfae lord who is a bridge between the Western and Eastern cultures. Two days prior to this, another healer shared with me that I was a bridge between the dimensions and can help others connect back to the true source of their soul and their origins. This healer helped me to reconnect with my memories of the beginning of time. These memories will slowly come back. I saw the universe and a tree. She told me to look for my tree while in the meditative state. Before I left to go to Australia in February, a Star Magic healer saw a huge tree come into the corner of my healing room. I was later told that my tree was the baobab tree.

Sitting in the corner of the healing room, in the energy of the baobab tree, with my shamanic healing stone, a wand of selenite and my journal, I closed my eyes. I waited a few minutes and then realized it was time to learn more about the Dragon Realm. I got on the back of Red, my dragon, and sat on something that seemed like a saddle. I caught myself giggling and saying, "Wow." As I sat, Red and I started to bring healing energies and light for him, to help heal his body. Dragon's bodies have much longer lifespans than humans. My friend is as old as my soul. I was told that a 200-year-old dragon would be equal to 2000 human years. I knew that we would not be travelling on this day, as he was getting a chance to heal and rejuvenate.

While sitting in the space and energy of the tree and my dragon, images of the universe came to my mind. Not many, but it was a start. I saw and felt a huge white-light sword on my back. The sword is for healing and bringing in the light and love energy, and it protects me while travelling through the universe.

As the memory of travelling came to my mind, I wondered if we needed to be cloaked at times. Then I remembered: not all shooting stars or comets are falling debris. Some are cloaked dragons and their riders. We can travel very fast, and when in the heart, our light is extremely bright. I was also wondering about the sword and started to see it in 3D in a vision. The sword is not sharp at the sides; it is thick so that it will never break. The handle is made with the same material and feels like working with selenite.

Dragons have the ability and speed to travel to the other dimensions. They are like messengers and can transport medicines and tools. When a healer needs medicine from another part of the universe, this can happen faster with a dragon, and the medicine can be delivered safely with its original essence intact. Imagine a truck or boat transporting vegetables. The longer the truck or boat travels, the more the nutrients and/or the essence of the medicine decrease over time. The dragon can keep the medicine's essence pure and untouched by aging or toxins.

Dragons are real. As I write this book, there are many practitioners who are becoming in tune with this beautiful ancient energy that is returning to our consciousness. We, as humans, are learning again to be pure of heart and humble.

August 12, 2019

A dear friend sent me a message: *I think your name is "She Who Dances with the Dragons."* What an awesome message to wake up to. This is the same friend who worked with me and the dragons in another lifetime.

I had a new client on this day. When she was settled on the table, I blurted out, "Do you believe in dragons? Let's play." My two little dragons were ready to play. Halfway through the treatment, I saw them weaving a belt. They would not let me see it until they were done. Near the end of the session, the belt was revealed: it had the seven colours of the chakras and three metal decals. A gold star was at the back of the belt and two gold diamond-shaped decals were on each side. The dragons shared that it was for the client to work with and to remind her to keep her vibration high and her energy centres cleared.

August 16, 2019

I just found out that dragons' train to do humans' work, too. To watch two little dragons flying around doing acupuncture for your client is shocking, surprising, yet sweet to see and amusing to watch. At first when I saw the acupuncture needles, I was startled and worried about them being applied properly. But when I got a closer look, I could see that the needles were blunt and could not puncture the skin, and I breathed a huge sigh of relief. A knowing that they must learn the skill and have the puncture sites remembered before starting to practice with the sharper needles. At the end of the energy session, I asked the client if she had ever tried acupuncture. She told me that it was her line of work! My little dragon friends got to practise on a professional!

*   *   *

Being able to reconnect with our dragon friends in this lifetime is really magical. I am not crazy, just happy and excited to hear stories and share them. Do you see dragons? Hear them? Dream of them?

Be open to the beautiful realms that are here with us and you, too, can have some amazing adventures. What we call our imagination is a doorway to all the infinite possibilities for us to experience here on Mother Earth.

CHAPTER **8**

Akashic Records

Healing for the human body has been available to us since the beginning of time. From the planets we came from (Arcturus, Palladia, Sirius and many more), to the planet on which we now live (Mother Earth), there is an abundance of natural medicine available to us. Healing techniques came from other planets and galaxies and new ones were created here on Mother Earth. When humans came to Mother Earth, the healers already had healing skills that are in our memories and hearts, and they also gained the skills that come with the consciousness of the mind. Yet, many of us came to earth with the agreement that we would not be born here with memories of our home planets. Our memories would return at the right time.

Our lifetimes are recorded in the Akashic records—a universal library of the lives of our personal soul. These records show what we came in with and the skills we developed in different lifetimes and from different planets, as well as knowledge that was shared and taught among different societies. The records show who we were in each life: male or female, the age we experienced traumas or celebrations, what countries we lived in, what we accomplished, and what we were scared to do. These records hold a lot of information about our soul's journey.

I believe that we have two sets of DNA: soul DNA and bloodline DNA. Our soul DNA holds a high vibration with the essence of God-unconditional love for all, that is. This DNA shows how we evolved over lifetimes. The bloodline DNA holds the lineage of our current earth family and shows how dynamics were created and if our families have seen anguish and/or sickness. We can also hold past-life trauma in our soul line. Sometimes we come into a family that will help us heal this trauma on the soul level. This healing can also provide healing for the family that we come into.

My soul originated in Arcturus, one of the oldest planets, which has technologies beyond our present comprehension. On this planet, we worked with the angels and honed our healing skills. This knowledge was brought to Mother Earth to help humankind in their evolution, along with other fellow beings from other planets who could assist in this process.

A fellow practitioner saw me in a vision as a female, on planet Earth, working with the herbs of the land. I was in a cave structure, and my connection with Mother Earth was strong. I was one of the first inhabitants here. I believe that this was in Australia, on the eastern coastline in the northern region. Or maybe it was in the Lemuria/Atlantis times. In 2016, during a trip to Australia, in the Kuranda Market, an Aboriginal land keeper greeted me and welcomed me to Australia. He shared that I came back home, to my mother country. This fellow had never met me before in this lifetime, yet he remembered me. What an honour this was to hear and to be greeted so lovingly.

So far, I have seen in my Akashic records, for my lives on Mother Earth, records of me being in Africa as a shaman, east Indian as a doctor, North America as a medicine man, England as a female psychic, Europe as a traveling psychic Gypsy and one of the first peoples in Australia, along with many others.

Working with the Akashic Records

During sessions with clients, I had started to see past lives from both this planet and other planets. I had taken a Past-Life Regression course several years ago. Doing regressions for clients was interesting, but there always seemed to be something missing. Once in a while, I would feel the energy from the clients, yet it was frustrating when the clients wouldn't pick up on it; it seemed as if the regression was not quite doing the job it should be. When I heard about the Akashic Record workshop, I knew that this was a must-do and that I shouldn't pass up this opportunity.

The woman who taught the workshop came up from the United States to teach it. She was guided to do the workshop for our group in one weekend and not two full weekends. She was concerned about this yet knew that this was the way the weekend was meant to be. We found out that all the students were Reiki practitioners, and all of us had experience and strong intuition. We were able to handle what she was teaching and met the requirements for each of the two levels.

While learning to work with the records, my body would heat up going into the energy, and then would cool down after each reading practice. I was finding that is was easy to see what went on in the lives of the people we practised on, and the details that the records were showing me were amazing. I also learned that when we are in the Akashic records, the healing is powerful and the stories and emotions or injuries that we hold on to due to a trauma has less impact the next time it comes up. It helps to heal the soul. We can also bring forward the skills and knowledge that we had in other lifetimes so that we can pursue our dreams with more ease and grace. Using the Akashic records, clients receive more information and feel the energy shifts a lot more strongly than when using the past-life regression method.

Gypsy Soul

During the workshop, a gal did a reading for me and she saw me as a gypsy. In this lifetime, I want to travel a lot more with my work as a healer/reader, in Canada and the rest of the world. This woman saw me as a gypsy travelling with a group of people and my twin sons (I saw these two boys in another lifetime, too). I was a very intuitive psychic who did readings as a living, but I was tired of travelling in that lifetime. I wanted my boys to stay in one place so they could grow up and have a stable life.

In this lifetime, I went to a lot of schools growing up, and I made sure that my daughters did not; they only had to move once while in school. When I was a young adult, I had the urge to travel, but I wanted to plant roots somewhere. When I went on the odd holiday, I remember the feeling of being a gypsy and wondered what it would be like to live that kind of lifestyle. It felt exciting.

What we got to do with the Akashic record reading, was to bring forth the gypsy soul part of me, to encourage me to travel and learn to feel free. The past-life me came forward into this lifetime and the urge to travel I have now is strong. I'm finding that I am taking more impromptu trips and camping again. I look forward to my next journey to Australia and hoping to go to Europe within the next five years. It was amazing to hear what the student in the workshop saw and the correlation to my life now. This made me believe strongly in this system of healing.

The Native Artist Within

As new readers of the Akashic records, it was highly recommended that we get in a lot of practice before charging for the sessions. One of my practice sessions was for a good friend who is an artist. For the life of me, I cannot remember much of the reading, but I do remember the native energy and the colour turquoise. I sensed that she was a Native American in another life, in Arizona. A person who loved to do artwork and beading. I just got an image in my mind of her beading a pouch for healing tools. I later found out from her that there is Native American lineage in her family.

Within a week after doing this Akashic record reading for her, my friend started to paint these amazing, vibrantly coloured dreamcatchers. I am so blessed to have one on my wall as a gift from her. She has sold quite a few of these beautiful and powerful pictures.

Not Being Able to Sleep (2017)

When we are not able to sleep properly, we run on empty and our bodies gets sick with colds and flus more often than others around us. One of my practice clients had been wondering why she could never sleep properly. She got maybe three to four hours of sleep each night.

We went into her records and were taken back to another life. In this life, she was a child in Europe and scared at night. During the night, bombs would be going off and family members would be huddled under tables and beds. No one really slept all that well and her fear rose each night. We sent lots of love to the little one in that lifetime and helped to heal her soul. We gave this past-life girl a huge energetic hug and told her how proud we were of her for being brave. This brought us to this lifetime and the lack of sleep, which started when my friend was about two or three years old.

Even though I'd known this amazing person for years, I did not know a lot about her. While doing the reading, I stopped at certain years in her life and shared what I saw. She provided an affirmation each time and was surprised at the accuracy of the timing and information. For each time that these events occurred, there was a healing of the soul.

Clearing in the Dungeon

I went to a client's home to do a house clearing in May. During the clearing, I could feel the depression and heart ache in the home. By mid-June, this person was still having a hard time and being attacked in her bedroom at nighttime. I had her come to the clinic to do an Akashic record healing to find out what was going on. During the reading, I had a flash-back to a vision I had of her before she came to town.

Two days before the clients' appointment, while driving my car to a friend's place, I asked Two Feathers, my guide, what was going on with this client. The word I heard was "psychotic." When I looked up the meaning of psychotic, it said:

"Having or relating to a serious mental illness that makes a person act strange; or that they believe things that are not true: relating to or suffering from psychosis."

Before I continue with this story, I need to explain something.

Over hundreds of years, people have been diagnosed by those who have no idea that there is something more around us. Spirits, entities, angels, fairies, the list goes on. If a person were to share that they saw these things, they would be diagnosed as being crazy and would not get the help that they truly needed to support the connection they had to the other realms.

Also, if a person is given drugs/prescriptions for ailments that their bodies are experiencing instead of properly looking after and healing the body, the medications can create hallucinations or can open the third eye more. This is something I believe can cause psychotic energy in a person, or it can come from being in extremely stressful and abusive relationships or serving in the war. It is okay for our third eye to open fully, but a person needs to learn how to discern what is good energy and what is not healthy energy. We need to learn how to set healthy boundaries with the spirit realm.

This client was exposed to something in a past life that caused a psychotic reaction and she had been on medication for migraines in this life. It led me to wonder what the medication was doing for her.

We did an Akashic record healing/reading for her to help find out what was really going on. Before the healing session, I had asked a friend if he could be there. He couldn't, but he checked in during the session. It is very rare that I ask for help. Later, I found out that this was something he needed to see, and I also needed the affirmation he provided later in the day.

During the session, the client shared that she had migraines, and that there was discomfort in her left leg. Discomfort on the left side of the body is connected with emotions. I was doing energy work on her body as we accessed her Akashic records. I was drawn to her heart centre, as that is where the energy on her leg was attached to.

In the records, I saw her in a dungeon. It had cement walls, or else huge bricks. This place was from another time, another life. Perhaps an old castle? During the reading, I saw her cowering in a corner, on the floor, crouched over and head down. I felt a lot of other energies, heavy ones, wispy black shadows floating in the room. I heard that this girl, in that lifetime, was being drugged with different concoctions to see what would happen to her mind. Would she see more? Would she see less? When she was targeted to do the experiments, whoever was in charge knew she was gifted with the sixth sense. These experiments caused her to go crazy and she become depressed and withdrawn. Psychotic, maybe? As we did energy work to heal the soul in that lifetime, the person in the dungeon slowly stood up and I finally saw a smile on her face. As we shifted her energy, we were also shifting the energy in the dungeon. I had asked both Archangel Michael and multidimensional Blue to help us out.

I was drawn to the room next to her in the dungeon. There was a guy in there, and I believe it was her brother. I got a strong sense that her brother was the reason that she was brought there in the first place. This person was very dark and lost. The energy of this person appeared as a dark, hairy parasite. I sent lots of Reiki energy to that room. When he came out, his head was hanging down and he had very long dark hair. Archangel Michael escorted him out. That soul still had a lot of healing to do.

Later that day, when I talked to my friend, he said that when he was guided to check in on the session, the first thing he felt was

Archangel Michael thudding into the clinic room where I was with the client. His energy shook the earth. Michael grabbed the bag that the client's brother was in and took it out. My friend shared that he saw the brother with long dark hair, just as I did. He also said that the face of the person appeared to be pointy, alien-like. It was a blessing to get his feedback and when he shared that Archangel Michael came in with such force, I realized why I was a bit anxious about working with the client, as we were dealing with something that was quite heavy and dark. But we did it! Archangel Michael, Blue, the client and I

Healing for the Client and Sister

This energy session in the Akashic records was amazing! The client went through a lot of emotions during the session and got to see why something was happening in this lifetime. When the session started, I had no idea that we were going to go into the records and never had worked with someone who could see so much while being in there. Another thing that shocked me was to see myself in there too.

At the beginning I saw myself sitting next to the client, I was her sister. We saw our own characteristics and how much we loved each other as sisters. During the session, the client gave me a play by play of the events that led to later in our lives. She went through a lot an anguish, and no matter how many times I tried to help I was deterred. The mother that we had at that time, is her sister in this lifetime. The challenge for her in this lifetime is with her sister, who was her mother in the past life.

The mother was very controlling and mentally abusive. I was able to get away and be with someone that I really loved. The client tried to get away too but had fallen off her horse and was caught. What she had endured after this was not pleasant. Later she was finally able to leave and came to the area of the country where I was with my partner. This lifetime ended amazingly.

When we look at the situation at another time and look at it again in this lifetime, forgiveness and unconditional love can be brought it to provide the healing. This time it was for both the client and her sister. Within 48 hours after the session, healing in the Akashic records provided a shift in both lady's life.

The Bindings That are Holding People Back

During many sessions, bindings show up. These bindings/ wrappings are like seeing an embalmed mummy that has been wrapped for burial. These bindings are showing us that an event occurred due to an accident or a personal attack. The bindings sometimes are only present on one area of the body. All the bindings that I have seen to date originated from past lives and I now know that I was accessing the records for information to help the client.

The last binding that I saw was around the waist of a client. I got the feeling that this person had obtained an injury in a past life to stop her from being a healer. Was this a stab in the back or a spear to stop the soul in that lifetime?

One binding I saw was to cover up an infestation of the energetic form of spiders, mentioned in Chapter 9. This was to hide what was going on and to maintain the lower energy form.

When these bindings are removed and the areas are energetically healed, the client can move forward in this lifetime. Not only will they be able to more easily pursue their dreams, they will not feel the discomfort in their body that they or the doctors could not find a cause for. All of this information can be found in the Askashic records and a person can be healed accordingly.

Areas of Armour/Patches

Sometimes, I will see a thick padding, armour or an energetic scar on a person. The areas are covered with thick energy and show that the body has been injured or suppressed in another life. During this energy work for the client, pictures come to me of the events, and it feels like the spirit of the person placed the armour there to protect the area, yet at the same time the armour did not allow for full healing.

The last armour/patch of energy I saw was wrapped around the left side of the client. On the client's back were three huge buttons that held in this energy. As the armour/patch of energy was being shifted, using both the love and light healing energies, we brought in the violet flame to empower that shift. Once the armour turned from dark to light, it was unbuttoned, removed and placed in a white netted bag that Archangel Michael looks after for me.

*   *   *

The Akashic records are a powerful way to help heal the human body. There is only unconditional love there and compassion for all those who are seeking the help of the records. Judgment has no place here, only the option to heal and learn from our previous experiences. The light beings that I see sometimes during sessions are the keepers and protectors of the records.

Chapter 9

Other Stories of Working between Dimensions

Over the years, I've gotten to experience and see a lot of amazing things on both this planet and in the other realms. Some of it I am still unsure about and don't know where the origins of these things are from. Some are created here on Mother Earth and some come from other galaxies, time and space. There are infinite possibilities and origins that humankind is finally starting to acknowledge again.

As a holistic practitioner, I find it is magical when we can help our clients shift from an unhealthy state of well-being to a state of freedom and happiness. It really is the client who is doing 90% of the work, and, as the practitioner, we get the honour of being there and helping unhealthy blocks transmute to love and light, or helping unwelcome energies do the same. When these energies are shifted back to the light/love state, we have helpers that escort them out for what I call "further processing." Maybe they are returned to their origins—I really don't know. This is for the higher-ups in the universe to look after. As practitioners, we do the groundwork.

Working with Heavy or Lost Energies

In my first book, *The Essence of Who We Are,* I talked about energies and spirits, light ones, and those who are lost or have become dark.

There are instances when energies are created to cause disempowerment. This could be anything from demon energy to greys, to automated energies that will not stop trying to harm all that comes in their way. These energies are on a mission to control and decrease the light and love vibration on the planet. From 2012 to now, I've seen many of these energies showing up during treatments, and some have been passed along timelines connected to past lives. Others are passed down through family bloodlines.

Our soul can have experienced many lives on different planets, including Mother Earth. These lives do not always have a human bloodline that is passed from family to family. Yet, at the same time, a soul in one lifetime can be affected by something, such as a heavy energy/contract, that is passed along a human family bloodline. Or the soul of a person can be very pure, and one that is not of the light may try to stop this beautiful soul from doing well. I would like to share some more experiences of working with these energies.

Following are some of my experiences in the healing room and classroom.

The Arcon

Toward the end of the morning during a Reiki class, a student noticed something on his friend's back. He said something about his friend's shirt moving. I thought it strange but didn't dismiss it, thinking that I would have to pay attention later in the afternoon. We finished our practice work with the chakras and stopped to have lunch. After lunch, the students split up into two teams, and they started to work on each other, practising working with the Reiki energy.

I was able to stand back and watch the students practise. My attention was drawn to the back of the one student, as it seemed as if his shirt really was moving. I watched the fellow as he practised and realized that the movement of the shift was not dependent on his breathing and the shirt would come away from his back. I got a weird and freaky feeling. There was something attached to this fellow. I asked the entity to get off the guy's back and go sit on the room divider, as I really did not know what it was. I thought maybe it was the spirit of a monkey or something like that. This was new to me.

After a few minutes, this energy was back on the student and his shirt was really extending out from his back, as if trying to prove a point and thinking it did not have to go. Got a bit nervous again. I started to do energy work on the fellow, bringing in the white light, and asked for help from both Archangel Michael and my guide. I kept on doing the Reiki until the energy form diminished and it was taken out for further processing by Michael. Shortly after that, the students traded partners to practise on. About half an hour later, it was this guy's turn to practise the Reiki again. After the session, he shared that his back was not hurting anymore, his energy was stronger and so was his intuition.

I figured out that the energy form that was attached to him was sucking in all the heavy energy that was coming from the energetic releases during the reiki sessions. What was not good was that the host (the student) for this energy form felt lethargic and experienced a lack of intuition. The energy was feeding off both the host and anything around it. After the workshop, I shared what I saw and praised the fellow's friend for seeing this energy form at the beginning of the workshop. I told them both that I had no idea where something like this came from but to be aware of where they go and to do a clearing of their energy fields if they feel something is not right. I asked a fellow practitioner a few days later what this negative energy thing was, and he told me it is called an arcon, and that it is not a good form of energy. It was a relief to know that I did do right by having it taking out by Archangel Michael.

The Spiders: 2017 to 2019

Spider Story I

I had one client who had me both confused and I was questioning myself if what I was doing was good, and if I was even capable of being a practitioner; I did not in any way want to be called a fraud.

This fellow gave me a call and said he wanted to do the Reiki as he was experiencing depression and found it hard to work. I felt uneasy at first, as once in a while, working on a male can leave me feeling hesitant—just a safety thing that comes to mind—then I need to remind myself that the angels and my guides will keep me safe. The Reiki session with this fellow went well and I enjoyed talking to him. Both he and his wife were from a region that sounds amazing, but I remembered him saying that there was good and bad medicine there. He had wondered if he had been sent bad medicine. This thought was put at the back of my mind and I did my best to clear his energy field.

He came back again and said that he was good for a few days after the first Reiki session, then it felt like there was a clamping on his head. During the session, there were again a lot of yawns, which are energy releases, and I asked the spirits that if there was any curse or anything like a curse on this fellow, that it be removed. Nothing showed up and the session seemed to go well.

The third time, his wife came with him and she also got a Reiki session. What an amazing woman. So kind and gentle, like the fellow that I was working on. The clamping came back for the fellow and again we worked on his head and the rest of him. When he called the fourth time, I was concerned.

His wife came again. This time she sat in a chair in the healing room, as she really enjoyed the energy in there. I said to both of them that this was crazy. How could this clamping keep coming back? I felt mad and wondered what I was really annoyed at. Was it the client? Was it myself? Why did I feel so angry that we were not getting anywhere with these sessions? It was very rare that it took more than a session or two before a person really started to feel a huge shift in their life. With being annoyed like this, I knew we needed to get to the bottom of this situation, and we started the Reiki session on the fellow. This is when I experienced something that I will never forget, and the same energy came in with another client a couple of years later: I was introduced to the spiders. This is not a good thing.

I always start at the head of the client and work down toward their right side before working on the left side—just a sequence that I go through. When I got to this fellow's stomach, I was drawn to do something I had never done before. I was told by the spirits that I needed to energetically open his stomach—like open two flaps to reveal what was inside. Suddenly, in my mind's eye, I could see hundreds of baby spiders coming out of him. I thought I was off my rocker and going crazy. Right away, I asked Archangel Michael to gather up these spiders and take them out. I placed the energy of the violet flame in his stomach to dispel any lingering spider energy. Then I was drawn to the top of the client's head and saw the huge mother spider. Immediately, we brought in the white light to energetically shift and change the field of this spider. That was the only way we were going to be able to get it to release so that Archangel Michael could take it away. Once this was all done, again I brought in the violet flame to further the healing process. Shortly after the mother spider left, I asked my spirit guide what this was really all about.

I was told that these spiders were supposed to be gone by the early 1900s. This was not good medicine. I contacted my fellow practitioner friend and asked him what this was about. He told me that I had heard right: the spider energy was brought in by a group of people who wanted mind control over their congregation or subjects.

This energy could be spread through voodoo lines or those practising bad medicine. He said that this energy would be gone within a few decades. This, I was relieved to hear, as it confirmed that I was not off my rocker and that what the universe had showed me was real.

Spider Story II

About a year later, I met a practitioner who was going through a rough time. After a few sessions with her, we found out that there was spider energy in her field. This, again, was from a form of mind control that was coming from a group of people in the area. What I realized was that she, like the fellow that I worked on previously, had layers of healing to do in order to get to the root cause. As we got through the layers, the truth was revealed, and the energy work brought in huge shifts and changes for them. These old energies and mind-control methods are not working as well in the new energies that Mother Earth is now supporting.

We were able to go to the source of where the spiders were originally coming from and prayed that the universe was able to look after it in a divine and fair way. It is magical to know that we can participate in changing the old energy fields and see less of it lingering. As each spider is changed, the collective of this energy is decreasing.

The Hairy Suction Cup Creature

It took about three to five days for this one to show up after the initial event. I thank God that I had a witness.

My friend and I were walking down a path in the neighbourhood. It was sometime in February or March. It was cold out and there was still some ice on the pathway, but not much. We were walking side by side and chatting. Suddenly, we both heard a huge crack, turned toward each other, and I asked him, "Did you hear that?" He did. I stopped on the path as I got a weird feeling that something just broke through the veil—and what it was, was not nice. In my mind,

I could see someone (in the form of a spirit of some sort) at the end of the path, and I did the energy work needed to escort what it was out with Archangel Michael. I did not hesitate or ask questions, because it felt like this spirit energy was not supposed to be here as it broke through the veil. Where did it come from? This energy work took some time and I noticed that my friend had gone a bit farther up the path and had stopped, too. I shared what I saw and the energy work that I was drawn to do. He said he saw a fellow with his head down. The spirit would not look at him. He, too, worked to help the spirit be escorted out.

When we got home, within a few minutes we realized something came home with us. My partner saw something in the bedroom and this time it was a female spirit, the same thing, head down and would not look at him. He helped that one to shift energy and had it safely escorted out. When I asked my practitioner friend again for feedback, he shared that some negative spirits are either trying to teleport or trying to come to the earth as a last resort. We caught these ones. Divine timing. I realized a day later that I did not repair the tear in the veil and prayed that nothing else came through. Right away, I did the repair work energetically and prayed for the best. Something else did come through, however.

We went for another walk in the neighbourhood and we were on our way home when something jumped on my friends' back. What I saw was a hairy sloth-like thing with suction cups on its feet. It looked and felt very intimidating and mean. It had round feet like small wheels. Imagine the end of a gun that has several holes in it that shoot out bullets. My friend said he felt something like shrapnel go into his back and he had to energetically remove every piece of it. The energy of this really hit him hard and we both worked to clear his back and energy field. The creature was safely escorted out, and we both knew that it came through the veil when we heard the loud crack. Again, we asked the angels to help round up anything else that may have gotten through and dispose of what they found. Thank goodness we didn't pick up anything else from that breakthrough of the veil.

Contracts

Story I

I mentioned contracts in my first book, and since they have been showing up a lot during sessions I have decided to revisit this.

During one house clearing, when I arrived at the office of the home, I saw a contract that the client either made or that was made on his behalf. When contracts are made energetically in past lives or between lives, they are not always done with good intentions. We are coming to a time when the energy of these contracts is no longer being supported by the energy field of the planet, and humans need to be able to feel free to grow and do well in their present lives. We are doing tons of energetic work on ourselves and for others around us so that we heal our lives in the past and present.

When I saw this energetic contract, I asked the homeowner about it and if he wanted it gone. With his permission, we asked that it be dissolved so that he could now flourish and that his hard work could be successfully abundant. The contract started to burn from the south-east corner up toward the top west corner. I watched it energetically burn until all the paper was gone. When I shared how the paper burned, the homeowner shared how the placement of Feng Shui in the office was the same as the direction of the burning of the paper. I was surprised again, as sometimes I still wonder about what the spirits show me. Right after this energy clearing, my client's life took an amazing shift for the better and the doors started to open for him again.

Story II

In July of 2019 a good friend sent a message looking for some help. I called her, both her and her family were getting zapped again by a rash of yucky events and it was hitting all of them financially. The oldest daughter was depressed again, and there was repairs to be done that should not be happening all at the same time. Did an impromptu clearing for the daughter. Then I asked spirit what was going on in the family. Suddenly I started to explain to my friend that both her and her oldest daughter had spent many lives together. They both had good and tough times in these different lives. This is the reason why they were still together in the same family. Suddenly I saw three to four contracts. The first one being the same as the contract in story one, this being finances, and watched this contract burn from corner to corner. This paper was white. The second contract was on red paper. Watched this one and the other one or two contracts behind it dissolve energetically. When this was done, there were no more contracts. Asked my friend to call me back in 2 – 3 days if things did not shift and I would come out to her place to do some energy work. So far not a word, as she only calls when things are not right and at her wits end.

In conclusion to contracts:

We can let go of contracts that are no longer serving us. A good friend did some research on the legalities of contracts, she found the information that supported what I was feeling.

A contract can be voided when both parties are not holding up their end of the agreement. When one party has done everything in his/her power to bring resolution, and the other party continues to abuse its part, the contract can be voided.

Once a contract is either voided or concluded, the person that is aware of the contract is now free to go forward.

Shifts in Energy Fields

Have you ever walked or driven somewhere, or even just sat in a chair and wondered where you went to, energetically?

Have you seen the energy shift, as if you just entered another energy field?

Have you seen through the veil?

During a visit with my daughter, we were sitting outside enjoying the weather and doing some artwork. Suddenly, I had a strange feeling, as if I had drifted off in thought, and then my daughter spoke up. She was shaking her head, as she shared that she saw me through a ripple in the energy. What she saw really startled her. Neither one of us could figure out what we saw. Did she see me working in another dimension or timeline? I have seen the same ripple in the energy field, it is amazing to see. Appears as waves of energy floating in the air.

There are the odd times when I can feel a shift in the energy field, and I know something is about to change. It feels like being in two places at once. Being here, but not being here.

One evening while spending time with a friend, he saw white light coming from my eyes. My eyes had changed shape to an almond shape. Shortly after that, I saw rainbow sparkles around his face! This brought a sense to both of us that we had a deep soul connection. We were seeing each other in another dimension.

If you ever experience any of these things, write them down and keep track of what you are seeing. After a while, you will find that you are connecting on a much deeper level to the other realms.

Be careful, and make sure that you are staying grounded, working with those who walk in the light and that you are connected to Mother Earth.

Using the Violet Flame

Over the past several years I have had to bring in the violet flame during the odd treatment. As my intuition has grown stronger, I started to pick up more on what the violet flame was doing, and how transforming it was for energies that were harder to shift and release from a client's energy field.

In August 2019, energy shifts were being shown to me, especially when parasite-like energies were being released. There was one energy that had taken root in a client. As soon as we brought the violet flame around the root and under it, the shift was instantaneous. When I did this again for a heavy energy parasite, the release of this parasite happened fast. It was as if it jumped out of its host and went straight into our bag of white light for further transformation.

*   *   *

I have learned many lessons and had many incredible experiences in this lifetime, and I know there are many more to come. We, as lightworkers, need to stay in the heart space and know that our love and the love from God/Creator is pure, unconditional love. This love is so strong that it can transmute the heavy energies on this earth.

I also try to remember that I am not responsible for the outcome of the energies or beings that Archangel Michael and Blue escort out. This is up to the Law of the Universe. Things like contracts, spiders, arcons, parasites or other energies that are not of the light and are being used to manipulate or control humankind are no longer acceptable. These energies must be escorted out. The love and light energies that are returning to Mother Earth are the most loving and powerful energies known in the universe. These energies and those who use them will be met with unconditional love and shown how to return to the light. They will learn again what it is like to operate in the heart centre, and that control is no longer needed or accepted on the Earth plane.

As a person who is not in the healing field, there are so many amazing things that you can see if you open your mind and your heart to the possibilities. I f you are interested in opening up to other realms, always ask to walk in the light and know that you are protected. If something funky and unsettling happens, get a qualified practitioner to help you out right away.

*   *   *

Remember that you are a beautiful soul!

We can all find the tools for healing in physical plain and on a Multidimensional Level.